Joyce and
the Law of
the Father

Frances L. Restuccia

Joyce
and the
Law
of
the
Father

Yale University Press
New Haven and London

Set in Sabon type by David E. Seham Associates, Inc.,
Metuchen, New Jersey. Printed in the United States of America.

Library of Congress Cataloging-in-Publication Data

Restuccia, Frances L., 1951–
  Joyce and the law of the father / Frances L. Restuccia.
  p. cm.
  Includes index.
  ISBN 0-300-04444-5 (alk. paper)
  1. Joyce, James, 1882–1941—Criticism and
interpretation.   2. Joyce, James, 1882–1941—Knowledge—
Psychology.   3. Fathers in literature.   4. Patriarchy in
literature.   I. Title.
PR6019.09Z78437   1989   88-39658
823'.912—dc19   CIP

The paper in this book meets the guidelines for permanence
and durability of the Committee on Production Guidelines for
Book Longevity of the Council on Library Resources.

10   9   8   7   6   5   4   3   2   1

To my mother and father

"Fac ut portem Christi mortem,
Passionis fac consortem,
    Et plagas recolere.

Fac me plagis vulnerari,
Cruce hac inebriari,
    Et cruore filii;
Inflammatus et accensus,
Per te, Virgo, sum defensus
    In die judicii.

Fac me cruce custodiri,
Morte Christi praemuniri,
    Confoveri gratia.
Quando corpus morietur,
Fac ut animae donetur
    Paradisi gloria."
—*from Jacopone da Todi, "Stabat Mater"*

Contents

Preface

This book situates itself at the crossroads of several Joycean controversies. Yet it might be seen as less disputatious than that description would suggest if its attempt to account for antithetical critical positions is considered. Not that *Joyce and the Law of the Father* is the product of mixing opposed perspectives until they formed some bland solution. Rather, in the spirit of Barbara Johnson's work, I have tried to locate the differences of critical opinion within Joyce's writing. Some feminist critics, for example, read "Penelope" as retrograde, as offering a resolution, the very notion of which the rest of the text seeks to undermine; others wish to celebrate the chapter as a culmination within *Ulysses* of *écriture féminine*. Both characterizations derive from "Penelope," and Gilles Deleuze's work on masochism, which I have extended to the vicissitudes of Joyce's writing, allows one to see why both mastery—authorial control as well as a kind of unified vision—and "woman's writing" emerge in that final chapter.

This leads to another sensitive matter. The present study makes heavy use of Deleuze's 1971 essay called *Masochism: An Interpretation of Coldness and Cruelty* because the theory that Deleuze generates through his careful analysis of Leopold von Sacher-Masoch has explanatory power for Joyce. Had I been able to apply Deleuze's theory of masochism only to Joyce's life, I would not have pursued the project. But Deleuze's insistence upon the grounding of masochism in the formal elements of Masoch's writing led me to observe a masochistic strategy within Joyce's writing that enabled Joyce to work toward liberation from patriarchy, in particular Church patriarchy. Wary of the reductiveness of psychologizing, I might at this point, then, have abandoned my discovery of the compatibility between Joyce's "real-life" masochism and that of Masoch. Yet not only did my sense of Joyce's enactment of masochism reinforce my sense of his writing's enactment of it, but Deleuze's stress on the inextricable relation of "real-life" masochism and what might be called literary masochism led me to retain a focus on both areas, never taking one as the cause or catalyst of the other. More than this, one must of course keep in mind that any evidence of "real-life" masochism comes to us only through language—in the case of this study, primarily through the texts of Joyce's letters and Ellmann's biography.

Readers who have familiarized themselves with Deleuze through *Anti-Oedipus: Capitalism and Schizophrenia* and subsequent works may be surprised by the emphases of my so-called Deleuzean angle on Joyce. Deleuze has vehemently challenged Freudian concepts such as the Oedipal complex, castration anxiety, and the (more Lacanian) law of structure and lack, some of which he appears to keep alive in his work on Masoch. So one simply may feel the need to distinguish earlier from later Deleuze. Yet the Masochian/Deleuzean theory of masochism has its own anti-Oedipal strain, in another sense. Already in *Masochism* Deleuze is interested in the masochist's getting beyond Oedipal guilt by ousting the father. What is negative engagement with the Oedipal theory, a position against it, becomes in *Anti-Oedipus* an attempt at obliteration of it: Deleuze realizes that the only freedom from the Oedipal complex is total repudiation of the concept itself. And there is at least one other striking link between Deleuze's work on masochism and later writing. In "How Do You Make Yourself a Body without Organs," in *A Thousand Plateaus:*

Capitalism and Schizophrenia, Deleuze includes an imaginary masochist's dramatic nine-item request to a mistress for physical (typically Masochian) punishment. It appears to be a masochistic "program" meant to stamp out the father Freud, to break down the "phantasy" of psychoanalysis and the phantasy-generating capacity of psychoanalysis. The masochist "uses suffering as a way of constituting a body without organs and bringing forth a plane of consistency of desire." The antipatriarchal strategy of *Masochism,* with some qualification, in other words, could be (in a sense, in *A Thousand Plateaus,* is) put in the service of canceling Freud. But I say "with some qualification" because in *Masochism* Deleuze allows himself to overlap with Freud (he adopts, for example, Freud's ideas on the fetish) in a way that later would be impossible. The theory of masochism has been emptied of all its psychoanalytic trappings, the only way of course that it could sabotage psychoanalysis itself.

For the most part, however, Deleuze—like Joyce—distances himself from Freud even in the essay on masochism. And perhaps Joyce even moves, like Deleuze, from a less radically antipsychoanalytic literary universe (in *Ulysses*) to a fuller refutation of psychoanalysis (in *Finnegans Wake*). A reading of *Finnegans Wake* against *Anti-Oedipus* and its sequel, *A Thousand Plateaus,* is the next step this study would have taken had it earned at least one more Mellon fellowship. I leave it to another masochistic soul.

Perhaps finally there needs to be an attempt at a justification for reexamining the Bible and Catholic Mysteries, topics that some poststructuralist criticism of Joyce has chosen to elide. (Beryl Schlossman's *Joyce's Catholic Comedy of Language* is a fascinating exception.) Yet no one reads Joyce well without noticing how loaded his writing is with theological subject matter. More important, the shift in Joyce away from patriarchy and toward poststructuralist strategies is predicated on a desire to break his allegiance to the Church (which is exactly where the Masochian/Deleuzean theory is so useful). In other words, Joyce's poststructuralism is based in his intricately entangled relationship to Catholicism so that a study of Joycean textuality that ignored the Church would miss the point. As Derek Attridge and Daniel Ferrer write in their introduction to *Post-structuralist Joyce:* "It is not possible to dismiss altogether meaning, character, and referential value. The full strength of Joyce's text cannot be appreciated if one does not differentiate it from a psychotic shout or a poetical incantation. It acts from *within* the Great Tradition of narrative fiction, violently dragging that tradition out of itself. It is as the culmination of Western culture that it leads that culture irretrievably astray, far towards the limits of madness." For these reasons, I have restored material that some might regard as passé. But since rebellion against Catholicism constitutes in Joyce's case the movement to, what I call for brevity's sake, textuality, I cannot see how the Church can possibly be left behind.

Acknowledgments

I would like to thank Professor Richard Hunt, the Director of the Mellon Faculty Fellowship Program at Harvard University, and the Mellon Foundation for providing me with a fellowship for 1987–88 to complete this project. Professor Marjorie Garber's efforts in running the Center for Literary and Cultural Studies at Harvard guaranteed that my year off was stimulating and intellectually rich in ways that contributed vitally to my work. Because *Joyce and the Law of the Father* has been coming to fruition for a few years now as well as because of its interdisciplinary nature, I have gleaned information and ideas from sources too numerous to specify, but I wish to thank heartily all teachers, colleagues, and students (especially at the University of California at Berkeley, the University of Wisconsin at Milwaukee, Harvard, Williams, and Boston College) who have contributed. Finally, deepest thanks to John Limon.

Acknowledgment is also due to those journals that allowed me to use the following articles in revised form: "Not Foreknowledge, Simply Knowledge: Secular Typology in *Ulysses*," *James Joyce Quarterly* vol. 20 (1983); "Wordplay: God and Pun in *Ulysses*," *James Joyce Quarterly* vol. 21 (1984) (coauthored with John Limon); "Transubstantiating *Ulysses*," *James Joyce Quarterly* vol. 21 (1984); and "Molly in Furs: Deleuzean/Masochian Masochism in the Writing of James Joyce," *NOVEL: A Forum on Fiction,* vol. 18, no. 2 (Winter 1985): Copyright NOVEL Corp. © 1985. Reprinted with permission.

Abbreviations

D Joyce, James. *Dubliners: Text, Criticism, and Notes,* ed. Robert Scholes and A. Walton Litz. New York: Viking Press, 1969.

P Joyce, James. *A Portrait of the Artist as a Young Man: Text, Criticism, and Notes,* ed. Chester G. Anderson. New York: Viking Press, 1968.

Exiles Joyce, James. *Exiles.* New York: Viking Press, 1951.

U Joyce, James. *Ulysses,* ed. Hans Walter Gabler. New York: Random House, 1986.

Ellmann Ellmann, Richard. *James Joyce,* new and revised ed. Oxford: Oxford Univ. Press, 1982.

SL Joyce, James. *Selected Letters of James Joyce,* ed. Richard Ellmann. New York: Viking Press, 1975.

Joyce and
the Law of
the Father

1

From Whip
to Reed

*The Ruler of the universe entreated
you, a creature of clay, to love Him
Who made you and to keep His law.
No. You would not.*
—Father Arnall, *A Portrait*

*My mind rejects the whole present so-
cial order and Christianity—home,
the recognised virtues, classes of life,
and religious doctrines.*
—Joyce, *Selected Letters*

Whipping seems to have made a deep impression on
Joyce's psyche. In 1904, Joyce wrote to Stanislaus about
Nora that

she used to go with Mulvey (he was a Protestant) and walk
about the roads with him at time[s]. Says she didn't love
him and simply went to pass the time. . . . Her uncle got
on the track. Every night he would be at home before her.
"Well, my girl, out again with your Protestant." Forbade
her to go any more. She went. When she came home uncle
was there before her. Her mother was ordered out of the

1

room (Papa of course was away) and uncle proceeded to thrash her with a big walking-stick. She fell on the floor fainting and clinging about his knees. At this time she was nineteen! Pretty little story, eh? [*SL* 46]

In a remarkable poem that Joyce sent to Stanislaus the previous year, his vision of the sadism surrounding him dilates phantasmagorically to an entire army of charioteers furnished with "fluttering whips":

> I hear an army charging upon the land
> And the thunder of horses plunging, foam about their
>   knees,
> Arrogant, in black armour, behind them stand,
> Disdaining the reins, with fluttering whips, the
>   charioteers.
>
> They cry amid the night their battle-name;
> I moan in sleep, hearing afar their whirling laughter.
> They ride through the gloom of dreams, a blinding
>   flame,
> With hoofs clanging upon the heart, as upon an anvil.
>
> They come triumphantly shaking their long green hair,
> They come out of the sea and run shouting by the
>   shore—
> My heart, have you no wisdom thus to despair?
> Little white breast, O why have you left me alone?[1]

The contrast in tone is too self-evident to require much comment—except to say that the poem may reveal how much nightmarish tumult is concealed in the laconic *Dubliners* flatness of the letter to Stanislaus. (The foam, fluttering whips, and blinding flame of the poem are hidden in the understated artfulness of "She fell on the floor fainting.") More important is that Nora's unprotected femininity turns out to be the only possibility of protection. From the beginning of Joyce's life, the only prospective savior he recognized within the sadistic atmosphere of his Irish childhood was female: if he started out yearning for a "Little white breast" to save him from violent men, later he would urge Nora to indulge him with larger ones. While Mark Shechner comments in *Joyce in Nighttown* that "the problem of the father in *Ulysses* is that he is missing"[2] and decades of Joyce scholarship have insisted on Joyce's/Stephen's craving for union with a spiritual father, it seems to me that Joyce had a surplus of fathers and surrogate fathers, that their presumed authority was the problem, and that Joyce exhausted himself in attempting to subvert the law of the father/Father to achieve the pleasure of Nora, Molly, Mary, and "Penelope." Women and their use of language were both Joyce's escape route and, in a way, his destination.

From the onset of Joyce's writing, Dublin emerges as a redoubtable punishing environment, as one father-figure after another seems to delight in the potentially castrating activity of whipping. In "An Encounter," the unforgettable bottle-green-eyed, yellow-toothed nameless pederast instills fear into the boy-narrator by relating to him his lascivious desire to whip young boys: "He said that when boys were that kind they ought to be whipped and well whipped. When a boy was rough and unruly there was nothing would do him any good but a good sound whipping. A slap on the hand or a box on the ear was no good: what he wanted was to get a nice warm whipping" (D 27). Whipping is the punishment of choice for crimes elaborated in a subtly discriminated code:

> He said that if ever he found a boy talking to girls or having a girl for a sweetheart he would whip him and whip him; and that would teach him not to be talking to girls. And if a boy had a girl for a sweetheart and told lies about it then he would give him such a whipping as no boy ever got in this world. He said that there was nothing in this world he would like so well as that. He described . . . how he would whip such a boy as if he were unfolding some elaborate mystery. [D 27]

What especially agitates and stimulates the pederast is the idea of a sexual encounter between a boy and girl. The pederast's brief visit to the near end of the field, an act that elicits the exclamation "I say! Look what he's doing!" (*D* 26) from Mahony, probably not an easily shocked observer, certainly suggests the "enormity" that Grant Richards and his printer missed.[3] He (like Nora's uncle) may be seen as an agent of sexual (at least heterosexual) repression—empowered to convert his threats into action, as he holds "a stick with which he tap[s] the turf lightly" (*D* 24). The pederast of "An Encounter" is the first in a long concatenation of potentially castrating father-figures flourishing in Joyce's fiction. He seems to be a sadist reaping sexual gratification from a beating fantasy.

Little Chandler in "A Little Cloud" likewise plays the role of the castrator; it is oddly as if he comprehends that in chastising his boy he hands down to him his own impotence (most of Joyce's sadists are actually pathetic and sexually insecure). From this story we gather that the Dublin male's fate is to be whipped, and subsequently to carry on the heritage of whipping—a tradition from which Joyce labored to extricate himself. (Though Nora spanked Giorgio and Lucia, Joyce refused to punish them.) Chandler is aligned with his baby boy, which assimilates castrating father with castrated son. He is, in the first place, "Little Chandler . . . a little man. His hands were white and small, his frame was fragile, his voice was quiet and his manners were refined. . . . The half-moons of his nails were perfect and when he smiled you caught a glimpse of a row of childish white teeth" (*D* 70). His wish "to assert his manhood" (*D* 80) belies the fact that he has any. Although Chandler does not literally whip his son, he gives him a verbal whipping with the lash of one angry, loud "Stop!" to terminate the child's wailing (*D* 84). When Chandler's wife, Annie, returns home to find her son screaming and comforts him with the phrases "My little man! My little mannie!" and, on top of this, *Chandler* sheds tears, the identification of Little Chandler with his little boy is complete. Chandler has shouted into a mirror of his own making; his "tears of remorse" (*D* 85) hint that he realizes, perhaps unconsciously, that he is an incarcerator himself in the prison of "dear dirty Dublin." The law of the father is insidious: it closes up escape routes quietly, forever reproducing even unwitting converts.

It is not just a few punishing fathers whom Joyce imagined as emasculating: they seem to infiltrate every Dublin household. A literal child beater, Farrington of "Counterparts" is also reflected in the mirror of his mistreated son. Mr. Alleyne, Farrington's boss, degrades Farrington: he threatens him— "Let me tell you that if the contract is not copied before this evening I'll lay the matter before Mr Crosbie" (*D* 87)—and humiliates him, by calling him names and shouting at him in front of Miss Delacour—"You impertinent ruffian! I'll make short work of you! Wait till you see! You'll apologise to me for your impertinence or you'll quit the office instanter! You'll quit this, I'm telling you, or you'll apologise to me!" (*D* 91– 92). ("Apologise, apologise!") Farrington's repressed violence, the result of Mr. Alleyne's treatment of him as well as of attendant humiliations during the course of the dreary day, must erupt, as it does, on his poor son. One link on the chain of the punished who in turn become punishers, Farrington is to Mr. Alleyne what his son is to him; faithful to its title, the story sets up two master/slave counterparts. At the end Farrington mimics his boy's flat accent ("*At the chapel. At the chapel, if you please!*" [*D* 97–98], the boy's innocent answer to Farrington's question concerning Mrs. Farrington's whereabouts), further identifying himself, through his mockery, with the child he beats. Like his son, Farrington can envision "no way of escape" from the world of beating (*D* 98): he strikes at the youth "viciously with the stick. Take that, you little whelp!" (*D* 98), enacting the pederast's obscene desire. Possibly Farrington experiences a sadistic release here, but, as the parallel with his son suggests, only at the cost of his potency. Joyce shows that the Dublin male's preoccupation with phallic power is the sign of its lack.

Dubliners alone contains at least three other stick-carrying members of the cast of castrated castrators. In "Eveline," Eveline's father used to hunt the children "in out of the field with his blackthorn stick" (*D* 36). Apparently Eveline still has reason to fear an outbreak of her father's rage: "She would not be treated as her mother had been. Even now, though she was over nineteen, she sometimes felt herself in danger of her father's violence. She knew it was that that had given her the palpitations. When they were growing up he had never gone for her, like he used to go for Harry and Ernest, because she was a girl; but latterly he had begun to threaten her and say what he would do to her only for her dead mother's sake. And now she had nobody to protect her" (*D* 37–38). In "A Painful Case," Mr. Duffy carries a "stout hazel stick" that he uses to strike "the ground regularly" (*D* 113), as if to unleash pent-up neurotic tension. (Duffy is self-castrating in his un-willingness to explore desire with Mrs. Sinico.) And in "Ivy Day in the Committee Room," Old Jack regards his old age as the only barrier to his taking "the stick" to his son's back and beating him, as he did in the past (*D* 120). (Though he doesn't carry a cane, Mr. Kernan in "Grace" had been violent, Mrs. Kernan reveals, before the boys had grown up [*D* 156], just as one night Mr. Mooney in "The Boarding House" "went for his wife with the cleaver" [*D* 61]. And if we widen our scope to *Ulysses*: Gerty MacDowell "had even witnessed in the home circle deeds of violence caused by intemperance and had seen her own father, a prey to the fumes of intoxication, forget himself completely" [*U* 290].) Older impotent men with the desire to emasculate usually younger, always weaker, victims seem general all over Ireland.[4]

And they pervade the Church, at least in Joyce's critique of it. Dublin fathers and Catholic Fathers comprised for Joyce the same hostile and oppressive milieu. In 1904, Joyce wrote to Nora: "Six years ago I left the Catholic Church, hating it most fervently. I found it impossible for me to remain in it on account of the impulses of my nature. I made secret war upon it when I was a student and declined to accept the positions it offered me. By doing this I made myself a beggar but I retained my pride. Now I make open war upon it by what I write and say and do" (*SL* 25–26). To avoid "emasculation," he needed to exile himself not only from his birthplace but from his religious vocation as well.

That both were threatening is conveyed by certain images in Joyce's writing that blend the perversity and oppressiveness of Ireland with the perversity and oppressiveness of the priesthood. Joyce's account of Nora's uncle taking a stick to her is immediately preceded in his letter by—and fused together in his imagination with—a description of a curate in Galway who "took a liking" to Nora: "One night at tea he took her on his lap and said he liked her, she was a nice little girl. Then he put his hand up under her dress which was shortish. She however, I understand, broke away. Afterwards he told her to say in confession it was a man not a priest did 'that' to her. Useful difference" (*SL* 45–46). The priest's half-lie (it was a man *and* a priest that did "that" to her) and Joyce's sardonic approval of it together manage to impeach the priest's manliness and make it an epitome of Dublin manliness in general. That Joyce affixes this story of the abusive curate to the other of the abusive uncle draws out the sexual perversion underlying the act of whipping (the curate's perversity is transferred metonymically to the uncle) as well as extends the range of potential sadists to the priesthood (the uncle's sadism is transferred metonymically to the curate). Joyce's juxtaposition of uncle and curate in addition aligns obliquely the pederast in "An Encounter" with the Catholic clergy: like the uncle who thrashes Nora and who is linked in Joyce's mind with the curate who sexually assaults her, the pederast craves whipping; and while the curate says that Nora is a "nice little girl," the pederast, as if mesmerized, tells the boys that "there was nothing he liked . . . so much as looking at a nice young girl, at her nice white hands and her beautiful soft hair" (*D* 26). Through their behavior and speech patterns, whipping uncle, sexually abusive curate, and perverted pederast, all get melded together.

Within *Dubliners* this alignment of priest and pederast is tightened. The word "queer" associates the pederast—"a queer old josser" in Mahony's vocabulary (*D* 26)—with Father Flynn in "The Sisters": Old Cotter speculates, "There was something queer . . . about [Father Flynn]" (*D* 9–10); and one of the priest's sisters echoes, "I noticed there was something queer coming over him latterly" (*D* 16). Like the pederast, Father Flynn has "discoloured teeth," and his habit of letting "his tongue lie upon his lower lip," which instilled uneasiness in the boy-narrator "before [he] knew him well" (*D* 13), invokes the sick old man. The suspicious way Old Cotter speaks about Father Flynn casts a perverse, illicit light on the priest's relation to the boy: "I wouldn't like children of mine . . . to have too much to say to a man like that. . . . It's bad for children . . . because their minds are so impressionable. When children see things like that, you know, it has an effect . . ." (*D* 10, 11). Apparently Cotter is vaguely right: in imagining the dead paralytic (his lips "moist with spittle"), the boy feels his soul recede "into some pleasant and vicious region" (*D* 11). Calling up the image of a priest chanting the Church liturgy, the pederast, in his verbal meditation on girls, gives the impression of "repeating something which he had learned by heart": "He repeated his phrases over and over again, varying them and surrounding them with his monotonous voice" (*D* 26). And one of the boys, Leo Dillon, had feared running into Father Butler or someone else from the college out at the Pigeon House, encouraging us again to impose the figure of a priest on the figure Mahony and the boy-narrator finally do encounter.

But the correlation between priest and pederast is best made intextually across *Dubliners* to *A Portrait of the Artist as a Young Man*. For, like Farrington of "Counterparts," priests in *A Portrait* live out the pederast's whipping fantasy. Mr. Gleeson, with his "long and pointed nails. So long and cruel" (*P* 45), is assigned to flog Corrigan, possibly along with Simon Moonan and Tucker; Father Dolan, notoriously, pandies Fleming and Stephen. Father Dolan's words flaunt his intoxication with the act of flogging: "Get at your work, all of you, cried the prefect of studies from the door. Father Dolan will be in every day to see if any boy, any lazy idle little loafer wants flogging. Every day. Every day" (*P* 51). He seems to long to flog habitually.

In these vignettes Joyce exposes the repressive patriarchal atmosphere of his childhood. From *Dubliners* to *A Portrait*, the repressiveness intensifies; the idea of punishment dominates the first three and a half chapters of *A Portrait*. The punitive nature of the Church seems to have infected the general atmosphere. For one thing Stephen is surrounded by sadistic classmates such as Heron, who strikes him with a cane on two occasions: once (in the spirit of the pederast) for his supposed involvement with Emma and, at an earlier time, for the "heresy" in Stephen's essay as well as Stephen's opting for heretical Byron over Tennyson. Heron has learned Father Dolan's "art" well: "Behave yourself! cried Heron, cutting at Stephen's legs with his cane" (*P* 81). The hell sermon is dedicated intricately to the punishment theme, deifying Dublin fathers/Fathers as God-the-Father: "God would not be God if He did not punish the transgressor" (*P* 133). And, of course, *A Portrait* opens famously with a threat of punishment as Stephen's mother and Dante (agents of the Church and patriarchy) berate him as a child, presumably for wanting to marry the cursed Protestant Eileen. Some form of sensuousness is no doubt the criminal provocation. "O, Stephen will apologise. . . . O, if not, the eagles will come and pull out his eyes." Stephen expands their threat ironically (as Don Gifford has

pointed out to me) into a Protestant song that reverberates
in his sensitive mind:

> *Pull out his eyes,*
> *Apologise,*
> *Apologise,*
> *Pull out his eyes.*
>
> *Apologise,*
> *Pull out his eyes,*
> *Pull out his eyes,*
> *Apologise.* [P 8]

Following this punitive song (the first instance in *A Portrait*
of chiasmus, a literary cross Joyce bears) is another, albeit less
ponderous, song of punishment. "Athy grinned and turned
up the sleeves of his jacket, saying:"

> *It can't be helped;*
> *It must be done.*
> *So down with your breeches*
> *And out with your bum.* [P 44]

One's suspicion that Athy's verse conceals a deeper, more
disturbed response to being pandied than mere joking is confirmed by the subsequent line: "The fellows laughed; but [Ste-
phen] felt that they were a little afraid" (*P* 45). Stephen at
least shows an exquisitely keen receptivity to the pandybat.
It is even as if he intuits, as he begins to participate in, the
eroticism behind the tradition of flogging ("the Medieval
Church was obliged to place controls upon self-flagellation
when too many monks discovered its delights"):[5]

> But what was there to laugh at in it? It made him shivery:
> but that was because you always felt like a shiver when
> you let down your trousers. It was the same in the bath
> when you undressed yourself. He wondered who had to let
> them down, the master or the boy himself. O how could

they laugh about it that way? . . . And though he trembled
with cold and fright to think of the cruel long nails and of
the high whistling sound of the cane and of the chill you
felt at the end of your shirt when you undressed yourself
yet he felt a feeling of queer quiet pleasure inside him to
think of the white fattish hands, clean and strong and gentle.
[*P* 45]

Joyce's vulnerability to inheriting the legacy of punishment
his many fathers/Fathers seem compelled to hand down to
him is hinted at through Stephen's sense of "queer quiet pleasure" in the priest's white, fattish, clean, strong, gentle yet
sadistic hands. Later, after sinning with the prostitute, Stephen
finds masochistically "an arid pleasure in following up to the
end the rigid lines of the doctrines of the church and penetrating into obscure silences only to hear and feel the more
deeply his own condemnation" (*P* 106). After Stephen con-
fesses, he inflicts upon himself a series of tiny tortures, bringing
each of his senses under "a rigorous discipline" (*P* 150). The
hostile, repressive society of Catholic Dublin begins to seduce
him; he seems on the verge of indulging in Church punishment.
In *Ulysses,* we even watch Stephen beginning to imitate Father
Dolan's punitive pedagogic method: "Tell me now, Stephen
said, poking the boy's shoulder with the book, what is a pier"
(*U* 20). (It is oddly as if Joyce means to show that, as Jane
Gallop suggests, there is "a certain pederasty implicit in ped-
agogy.")[6]
But the long, baroque story of how Joyce cancels out these
patriarchs and their anathematizing of play—with his cruel
sleazy fantasies, the pederast interrupts the boys' playing
hooky and condemns boys talking to girls; Eveline's father
hunts the children at play in out of the field with his stick;
and the priests of *A Portrait* prohibit all fooling around in
class—of how he turns their law upside-down, also com-
mences in *A Portrait.* The tool of whipping metamorphoses

into an at least potentially playful tool of writing, as the priest-
ly vocation gives way to the writerly.

The transformation of whip to wand or pandybat to pen is
allegorized in the Clongowes classroom, where the two activities of punishment and writing are interwoven. Having
broken his glasses, Stephen cannot write, so instead he listens
to pens scraping and watches Mr. Harford pacing "to and
fro making little signs in red pencil and sometimes sitting beside the boy to show him how to hold the pen" (*P* 46). Mr.
Harford's pencil—in all its official and violent redness—keeps
alive the authority of the master while lying figuratively somewhere between pandybat and pen. When Father Arnall enters,
displeased with the "scandalous" themebooks, and makes the
boys write them out again with the corrections, writing becomes synonymous with punishment, only a lesser form of it
than being pandied. Fleming knows this difference through
hard experience since Father Dolan pandies him for writing
"a bad Latin theme" (*P* 48). Threatening to return "Tomorrow
and tomorrow and tomorrow," Father Dolan urges the boys
to "write away" and pandies Stephen for not writing at all
(*P* 49). Hence writing can be both punishment ("incorrect"
writing is punished with "correct" writing) and avoidance of
punishment ("correct" writing in the first place keeps Father
Dolan at bay).

But not to write leads to being "maimed": after receiving
the blows of Father Dolan's pandybat, Stephen "drew back
his maimed and quivering right arm" (*P* 50). Though Stephen
worries a bit later about whether his excessive sexual exploits
have "maimed" his body or soul, Joyce seems to want to stress
that whereas pandybats are emasculating, visiting a prostitute
is not. "Instead the vital wave had carried him on its bosom
out of himself and back again when it receded: and no part
of body or soul had been maimed but a dark peace had been
established between them" (*P* 103). Stephen/Joyce appears to
have internalized the lesson that writing (the more sensuous—

the more feminine?—the less maiming) could soothe and save him, that he needed to produce a style of writing that would go beyond merely keeping Father Dolan at bay.

Consequently, after Stephen's vision of "a winged form," "a hawklike man flying sunward above the sea," after his realization that "he would create proudly out of the freedom and power of his soul, as the great artificer whose name he bore" (*P* 169, 170), he picks "a pointed salteaten stick out of the jetsam among the rocks" (*P* 170) and clambers down the slope of the breakwater. This "stick" bears a clear kinship to that of the pederast, that of Farrington, the blackthorn stick of Eveline's father, the stout hazel stick of Mr. Duffy, the big walking-stick of Nora's uncle, not to mention the pandybats of the fanatically flogging Fathers of *A Portrait*. (Daedalus himself, after all, is an ingenious mythic father.) Yet, because it seems to have been magically, primordially born out of Stephen's epiphanic vision, we are invited to take it as an emblem of Stephen's/Joyce's (ultimately antipatriarchal) art.

That association—of stick with pen—gains ground. A brief time later, as Stephen stands gazing at birds (avatars of Daedalus?) while resting on his ashplant, the ashplant leads him to think vaguely of "the curved stick of an augur," and this image gives way to his fear of "the hawklike man whose name he bore soaring out of his captivity on osierwoven wings, of Thoth, the god of writers, writing with a reed upon a tablet and bearing on his narrow ibis head the cusped moon" (*P* 225). Though Thoth, Egyptian god of the moon, wisdom, and learning, carried a palm branch, which Stephen's ashplant may be meant to resemble, the ashplant also resembles sufficiently the form of pen described in the passage—a reed—to justify thinking of it additionally as a "pen." We thus witness the transmutation of the stick, the emasculating implement of whipping, into the magical wand of the artist.

But we witness a temporary reversal of this transformation too, as Stephen, out of frustration in attempting to communicate with Cranly, "beat[s] the frayed end of his ashplant against the base of a pillar," and, a moment later, is found "beating the stone softly with his stick to hide his revery" (*P* 232, 233), presumably over the wispy passage of Emma Clery before him through the dusk. In these scenes perhaps Joyce resurrects the shadowy image of the pederast, allowing us to glimpse the dirty old man, with his beating fantasy and longing for young girls and boys, lurking within Stephen. (Lurking too within Joyce: the pederast resembles Father Flynn, whose first name is James.) As late as the end of *Ulysses,* Stephen is still using his stick/ashplant to do violence: his mother's post-humous nagging at him to "Repent!" goads him into smashing the chandelier of Bella Cohen's brothel, obliterating time and space apocalyptically (*U* 474). The stick/ashplant seems to oscillate between being destructive/punishing and creative/ liberating, and it is possible that Joyce never fully calmed that oscillation.

Rebellions are rarely unalloyed; some sort of deep-seated complicity with what one rails against commonly exists. No doubt every bitter statement from Joyce about Dublin in general and the Church in particular can be countered with praise. Joyce wrote to Nora that he was "sick, sick, sick . . . of Dublin! It is the city of failure, of rancour and of unhappiness" (*SL* 163), even as he paid a kind of homage to his hometown in writing to Stanislaus that he "would like to have a map of Dublin on [his] wall. I suppose I am becoming something of a maniac" (*SL* 124). Joyce believed "that to establish the church in full power again in Europe would mean a renewal of the Inquisition—though, of course, the Jesuits tell us that the Do-minicans never broke men on the wheel or tortured them on the rack" (*SL* 94), yet Mary Colum in *Our Friend James Joyce* testifies that she never knew "a mind so fundamentally Cath-olic in structure as Joyce's own, nor one on which the Church's ceremonies, symbols, and theological declarations had made such an impression." In her estimation "his whole mind showed the mental and moral training of the Church."[7] I offer these clashing commentaries, however, not to rehearse the popular notion that Joyce had an ambivalent or a love/hate attitude toward his many fathers/Fathers, but to propose that he felt uneasily and profoundly implicated in, indeed constituted by, their mentality. As a result, the form his rebellion took inevitably was a repudiation of his attachment, of his resemblance, to those fathers/Fathers (the culmination of his schooling, after all, was meant to be his joining their Jesuit ranks), which attachment and resemblance had first to be reconstructed (literarily) in order subsequently to be broken down. One does not become an apostate Catholic overnight.

But more needs to be said, by way of introduction, about the fathers/Fathers whose law Joyce felt driven to reproduce, transform, and finally dismantle. My argument is not that Joyce suffered from an Oedipal complex. I take him at his word when he writes to Harriet Weaver lovingly and guiltlessly about his recently dead father, John Joyce: "My father had an extraordinary affection for me. He was the silliest man I ever knew and yet cruelly shrewd. He thought and talked of me up to his last breath. I was very fond of him always, being a sinner myself, and even liked his faults" (*SL* 360–61). Breaking the law seems to have united real father and son. (Likewise, Stephen Dedalus, instead of following in the footsteps of his literary ancester Oedipus by killing his father and desiring to marry his mother, behaves anti-Oedipally by "killing" his [patriarchal] mother and "marrying" [at the end of "Eumaeus"] his [noncastrating] "father" Leopold Bloom [whom he then casually bids adieu]. Even Simon Dedalus mainly evokes Stephen's pity; as Simon says, he does not "believe in playing the stern father" [*P* 91]; he shares Stephen's view of the Irish as "a priestridden Godforsaken race!" [*P* 37].) Though Joyce resisted patriarchal authority wherever he found it, the "law" that inspired fanatical insurrection in him did not belong to his biological father, fellow-sinner and law-breaker.

But as Joyce's letters and *Dubliners* testify, it was honored by the ordinary, punishment-happy Dublin father. And since patriarchal power, authority, and cruelty were anathema to Joyce (even when he located them in himself), he denigrated those Dublin fathers and father-figures who attempted to exercise mastery, even as their feeble attempts betrayed their impotence. The law of the father in general, then, is the broadest circle of concern of this study (and I will continue to use a lower-case *f* to signify those fathers whose authority derives from the structure of the family). But it was the more genuinely potent religious Fathers—generators of patriarchal law/knowledge/vision, abusers of patriarchal power—who provoked Joyce into an entire lifetime of writing, a form of self-flagellation (we will see) that facilitated his release from their snares (an upper-case *F* will continue to signify those Fathers who derive their authority from the structure of the Church). He located the Father's law writ large in particular in the Church—where it was upheld by Church priests, the Church Fathers, Thomas Aquinas, and as Father Arnall in this chapter's epigraph reminds us, God-the-Father Himself. My emphasis therefore will be Joyce's response to Church patriarchy.

Joyce criticism generally has tended to soften Joyce's rebellion against the Church. His letters contain snide remarks against priests: about Ireland and the Irish, he wrote scathingly, "I see nothing on every side of me but the image of the adulterous priest" (*SL* 174). He resisted being married by a priest and opposed baptism for his children. He wrote that he was "incapable of belief of any kind" (*SL* 62) and regretted that his removal of himself and his progeny from the Church was "too slow" a process: "I don't believe the church has suffered vitally from the number of her apostates" (*SL* 109). He exclaimed in a 1904 letter to Nora: "How I hate God and death! How I like Nora!" (*SL* 27).

It seems that Joyce held Nietzsche's outlook that "the Church fights passion with excision (*Ausschneidung*, severance, castration) in every sense: its practice, its 'cure,' is *castratism*" and that he produced fiction that supports Derrida's assertion (meant in *Spurs* as an extension of Nietzsche's idea) that "Hostile to life, the Church is hostile thus to woman also who is herself life (*femina vita*)."[8] ("How I hate God and death! How I like Nora!") Not only does Stephen visit the prostitute to escape his Fathers, but in her arms he assumes the passive, feminine position. In some sense Stephen is drawn to women to become a woman. Rather than penetrating, he allows himself to be penetrated so that he may thereby abandon himself: "He felt some dark presence moving irresistibly upon him from the darkness, a presence subtle and murmurous as a flood filling him wholly with itself. Its murmur besieged his ears like the murmur of some multitude in sleep; its subtle streams penetrated his being. His hands clenched convulsively and his teeth set together as he suffered the agony of its penetration" (*P* 100). The girl embraces Stephen, while he "all but burst into hysterical weeping." She appears to French kiss him: "His lips would not bend to kiss her," but between her parted lips "he felt an unknown and timid pressure" (*P* 101). It is as if Joyce thought that by aligning himself with women and, more extremely, by assuming the female position he could best free himself from the Church.

It is in fact from a "female" position that Joyce textualizes Catholic theology in *Ulysses*. First he incorporates biblical motifs and structures as well as Mysteries and rituals of the Church into his fiction on the narrative level; then he turns them to metaphor. But he eventually works them to the excruciating point that they become literary tropes evacuated of all theological meaning. He acts on, proleptically, Lacan's injunction to "make use, but really use them up, really wear out those old words, wear them threadbare, use them until they're thoroughly hackneyed."[9] The textual status that Joyce accords the Catholic theology his writing is based on comes to serve as a crucial part of his subversion—since, as Roland Barthes devoted himself to showing, textuality supplants authority. Once textualized, even theology joins the conspiracy. As Colin MacCabe phrases it in *James Joyce and the Revolution of the Word*, "The struggle against narrative"—the battle that Joyce's appropriated theology becomes complicit in—"is the struggle against the father."[10] Joyce in the end turns Catholic theology against itself.

Ulysses begins, however, by epitomizing representational writing, or at least by posing as the paragon of realism, and in doing so reflects Joyce's confiscation and literary exploitation of the fathers'/Fathers' weapon: the phallic whip, stick, pandybat is reincarnated as a "masculine" pen. MacCabe writes that the "self-possession" of the so-called representational work "is predicated on the possession of the power of the phallus, a possession conferred by a radical miscognition of sexual difference and language" (MacCabe 107). Despite Stephen's cry for a nonphallic art—"O! In the virgin womb of the imagination the word was made flesh" (*P* 217), a cry that manifests Joyce's womb envy still within the rhetoric of Catholicism—Joyce's pen (in other words) is not "feminized" immediately, if it is at all. As Joyce critics from Ezra Pound on have noticed, it takes until approximately "Sirens" for *Ulysses* to launch its assault on narrative, its unleashing of what MacCabe calls "female desire": "the passage along the metonymy of signifiers . . . when the signifier is no longer under the domination of the signified" (MacCabe 127). Putting aside the question of "female desire" for now, a case could surely be made that even prior to "Sirens" *Ulysses* sets in motion chains of free-floating signifiers. But I would apply to roughly the first half of *Ulysses* what MacCabe claims is true of George Eliot's *Daniel Deronda:* "We can read the desire to transgress the law of the father but, at the same time, [there is] the constant disavowal of that desire through an appeal to reality" (MacCabe 24).

Joyce then preserves the patriarchy from which he extracts his pen so long as he writes representationally—a mode of writing that, again borrowing MacCabe's (Lacanian) vocabulary, "represses the only activity that can furnish a lasting liberation from the dominance of priest and king (priest and king being so many names for the signified)" (MacCabe 88). That Joyce rebuilds brick by brick the city of Dublin—the very locus of the early repression of "the impulses of [his] nature"—through his use of naturalistic detail clinches the point. Repressive style complements content of repression. But Joyce swings in *Ulysses* from a realism of one-to-one correspondences that guarantee the law of the father(s)/Father(s) to a Text of what at least appears to be "female excess" (a vexed feminist matter to be taken up later), where gaps between signifiers and signifieds leave room to breathe, are sources of joy. The laborious movement from realism to the freer play of the signifier marks Joyce's inching toward liberation from the fathers/Fathers.

In a massive submove within this more widespread fatherly writing gesture, Joyce further preserves patriarchy through his use of Catholic theology as subject matter, thus setting up the Catholic Fathers I have identified as the primary targets of his retaliating pen. Catholic theology in *Ulysses* is played upon and played upon within the text to the point that its significance evaporates. In this way Joyce divorces or pries loose the Father from His Name, thereby exposing his fraudulent status. The following pages will investigate Joyce's rigorous, taxing, at times mechanical, even painful, playing out, his textualization and demystification of biblical motifs and structures and dominant Church Mysteries—the Eucharist, Incarnation, and Trinity—as he strives to achieve the pleasure of the Text.

2

From Typology
to Typography

I

*Coming events cast their shadows be-
fore.*
—Leopold Bloom, *Ulysses*

*The doctors of the church, they
mapped out the whole theology of it.*
—Leopold Bloom, *Ulysses*

Although Erich Auerbach, who in *Mimesis* categorizes
Joyce as a *modern* realist whose work expresses an
"atmosphere of universal doom" characteristic of Europe
at "the time of the first World War and after,"[1] failed
to notice, one of the literary goals Joyce set out to reach
with his patriarchal pen was to join the ranks of Christian
figural realists. In a sense he was successful. But in the
course of extending this line, Joyce gets carried away—
carried away with the ink flowing from his ultimately
recalcitrant pen—so that a shift slowly takes place.

Ulysses, that is, at first offers itself as a modern sacred
text, as a text possessing, to quote Hayden White explaining Ricoeur, "*something like* that anagogic or mystical meaning which the scholastics defined as constituting the ultimate significance of religious discourse in

20

general," or, in yet other words, as a symbolic system (White again) "the referents of which are both themselves (this is the auto-referentiality thesis of modernism) and something extrinsic to themselves [such as] social reality."[2] In the modern sacred text, autoreferentiality substitutes for the anagogic, while referential language provides its worldly base. (Brook Thomas no doubt typifies most Joyce readers in commenting: "On the one hand, *Ulysses'* exacting realism invites us, as [Marilyn] French's title reminds us, to read the book as world. On the other, its reflexiveness warns us to read the book as book.")[3]

But in the course of its evolution as a modern sacred text, *Ulysses* gradually remolds itself entirely into a Barthesian Text (I have in mind here in particular Barthes's "enunciations" in his essay "From Work to Text" in *Image Music Text*), leaving realism behind. It is, in fact, largely through the process of evolving into the modern figural realist text that *Ulysses* redefines itself as a Barthesian Text: Joyce could not release himself from the grip the Fathers had on him in one blow but had to ease away. For him this meant reproducing them—literarily—which was concomitantly an articulation of his complicity in their habits of mind, in order in the long run to subvert their power and free himself from their clutches. The process might be thought of as Joyce's ritual of bidding the Fathers adieu. But before bidding adieu, he had to greet them, confront them, pay them a kind of final tribute. And so *Ulysses* provisionally takes its proper place (not at the end of Auerbach's modern realist line but) at the end of his Christian figural realist genealogy.

As Auerbach elaborates in *Mimesis*, figural realism begins in the Bible, comes to full fruition in Dante, and shapes the writing of Augustine, Gregory of Tours, medieval Christian drama, St. Francis, Boccaccio, even Rabelais, Montaigne, and Shakespeare. (Stendhal and Balzac are the chief forefathers of the completely distinct modern realist line.)[4] It is founded on the principle that "an occurrence on earth signifies not only

itself but at the same time another, which it predicts or confirms, without prejudice to the power of its concrete reality
here and now" (*Mimesis* 555). The figural view of history
discovers links in mundane events, but it is crucial to note
that the link is primarily neither chronological nor causal: the
similarity between, say, Moses and Christ is due to their
"oneness within the divine plan" (*Mimesis* 555). A type is
never the agent of its antitype; instead type and antitype com-
bined "signify," as Auerbach puts it, one thing. The typical
(horizontal) link between the two events reveals the vertical
link by giving evidence of God's plan. In "Figura," the whole
system is described as a kind of right triangle: the figural realist
views an earthly event "primarily in immediate vertical connection with a divine order which encompasses it, which on
some future day will itself be concrete reality; so that the
earthly event is a prophecy or *figura* of a part of a wholly
divine reality that will be enacted in the future."[5]

Of course had Philo, the Christian Gnostics, Clement, or
Origen established the final Christian outlook on the relationship of the Old Testament to the New, the history of figural realism would not have occurred. These theologians, in-
fluenced by Platonism, promoted allegorical (rather than
typological) exegesis. They read the Bible as an allegory of
spiritual truths, assigning a minor role, if any at all, to the
literal and lateral level; they dedicated themselves, instead, to
moral, theological, and mystical meanings.[6]

Whereas the bias of allegorical exegesis is Platonic, the bias
of typological exegesis as well as of at least approximately
the first half of *Ulysses* is Aristotelian. Even if one had not
come across in Joyce's notebooks statements that make plain
his attraction to Aristotle (in 1903, by reading Cousin's translation of Aristotle's *De Anima, Metaphysics,* and *Poetics,* Joyce
sheltered himself "from the sin of Paris, night by night" [Ell-
mann, quoting *Ulysses* 120]), or noticed explicit references to
Aristotle in Joyce's novels, the fact that he loads *Ulysses* with

sensuous phenomena would testify to his Aristotelian insistence upon the reality of things in the world. Joyce dramatizes his early allegiance to Aristotle through Stephen's well-known proof, however flimsy, of materialism as against idealism. Aristotle secured his knowledge of the existence of the things in the world (Stephen recalls) "by knocking his sconce against them." Stephen then proceeds to enact his own proof done in the style of Aristotle's (or Samuel Johnson's) crude test: he closes his eyes, and opens them to discover whether reality has vanished. When he sees that it has not, he concludes that it was "there all the time without [him]" (*U* 31). In accord with the results of his experiment, Stephen (his "ash sword" hanging appropriately at his side) becomes an avowed materialist, thus adopting the philosophical position manifest in the aggressive realism of *Ulysses*. Joyce at least begins *Ulysses* in the role of maniacal, phallic realist: he needed Stanislaus and his Aunt Josephine based in Dublin to ensure that he got every minuscule detail right, to guarantee that every literary signifier met with an authentic Dublin referent. This artistic stance was part of his legacy from the fathers/Fathers. Although detail is stressed, it is not at this point Barthes's "inessential detail"—decadent/ornamental/feminine detail. Instead Joyce begins with Naomi Schor's "good" rather than "bad" detail, which amounts to the distinction between figural realism and figural writing per se: "The bad detail is a good detail which has gone bad by completely detaching itself from its support to become an end in itself, a detail for detail's sake."[7] (Joyce moves to such fetishism, but first he deals in realist details of containment.)

Modeled on the principles of typology, *Ulysses* not only aligns itself with Christian figural realism by virtue of its referential language that is simultaneously self-referential, thus producing an "anagogic" level hovering over a literal base; but it specifically, architectonically, imitates the Bible, Auerbach's paradigm of figural realism. Horizontal as well as vertical typological structures pervade the book. Characters and events (including linguistic events) in roughly the first half of *Ulysses* horizontally prefigure and are fulfilled by characters and events in roughly the second half, just as persons and events in the Old Testament prefigure and are fulfilled by persons and events in the New. As for the vertical dimension of typology in *Ulysses,* the realistic foundation of the book may be seen in constant relation to a linguistic/anagogic dimension that might be imagined as poised above it, just as mundane activities presented in the Bible have their spiritual counterparts; *Ulysses* implicates Joyce in the same way that events of the Bible point to God.

Figural realism, then, is constituted by a linking if not quite a chain of signifiers: a type signifies horizontally an antitype that in turn becomes a type (as all signifieds may be said to revert to signifiers) that signifies vertically a heavenly antitype. At least until heavenly fulfillment occurs, the irreducible figurativeness of God's sign system is taken for granted, although never at the expense of the literal. Yet even though figural realism seems a step beyond mere realism in that it finds for every signifier a second signified and for the second signified one reappearance as signifier, the chain is quickly cut. The moment of closure is bound to come, although it is postponed up to the revelation of divinity. In the end signifiers are conjoined with single signifieds, the linkage of which testifies to a grand divine plan. Textuality is suggested but not embodied: typology looks two ways, back to the most promising of Joyce's patriarchal ancestors, who are nevertheless still patriarchs, and with qualification forward to Barthes.

Tertullian was the first to use "figura" to describe a prophetic event that foreshadows things to come. (The Latin *"figura"* superseded the Greek *"typos"* ["Figura" 15].) Tertullian saw, for example, "the naming of Joshua-Jesus" as "a phenomenal prophecy or prefiguration of the future Saviour"; the Passover as "a figure of Christ through the likeness of the saving blood and of the flock of Christ"; "the two sacrificial goats of Lev. 16:7 ff." as "figures of the first and second coming of Christ"; and Adam too as a *figura* of Christ, the sleep of Adam as a *figura* of the death of Christ, and Eve, as she is born out of Adam's wound, as a *figura* of the Church ("Figura" 29–30). For the most part, there was agreement among the Church Fathers on cardinal issues: "Adam, or again Moses the law-giver, in a real sense foreshadowed Christ; the flood pointed to baptism, and also to the judgment; all the sacrifices of the old Law, but in a pre-eminent way the sacrifice of Isaac, were anticipations of that of Calvary; the crossing of the Red Sea and the eating of manna looked forward to baptism and the eucharist; the fall of Jericho prefigured the end of the world" (*Christian Doctrines* 72). The list can apparently go on indefinitely. These are instances of the horizontal dimension of typology (we will come to the vertical shortly), since each case involves a figura that is "something real and historical which announces something else that is also real and historical" ("Figura" 29). Even though in typology the figure is often designated *"umbra"* (the English equivalent of which term— "shadows"—Bloom uses) or *"imago,"* and the fulfillment as *"veritas,"* nonetheless both are "concrete in reference to the things or persons which appear as vehicles of the meaning" ("Figura" 34).

This particular conception of prefiguration and fulfillment came to dominate the development of biblical exegesis in the Latin Church writers; but before it could, a reaction against allegorism had to take place. In Antioch, during the fourth and fifth centuries, three theologians, Diodore of Tarsus, Theodore of Mopsuestia, and Theodoret, took active parts in the fight for typology (*Christian Doctrines* 75–76). Practical illustrations of the Antiochene theology informed the sermons of the preacher John Chrysostom, who framed "the classic definition of a type as 'a prophecy expressed in terms of things' " (*Christian Doctrines* 76). Chrysostom brought out the point of distinction between forcing "allegory out of the history" and preserving "the history intact while discerning a *theoria* over and above it": he led the Antiochene school in believing that "the literal sense of the sacred narrative should not be abolished" (*Christian Doctrines* 76). Chrysostom is alluded to on the first page of *Ulysses,* as if to signal immediately Joyce's investment in figural realism. Mulligan "peered sideways up and gave a long slow whistle of call, then paused awhile in rapt attention, his even white teeth glistening here and there with gold points. Chrysostomos. Two strong shrill whistles answered through the calm" (*U* 3).[8] The name of this Father of typology sits stolidly between a call and its answering call.

Leopold Bloom himself seems naturally inclined to impose a secular sense of horizontal typology on ordinary events. In "Lestrygonians," the coincidence of his thinking of Parnell and then seeing Parnell's brother, and, on top of this, of thinking of A.E. and Lizzie Twig and then seeing them, prompts Bloom to think, "Coming events cast their shadows before" (*U* 135). One might even say that Bloom's interpretation of these incidents adumbrates a similar idea (itself couched in the terms of typology) expressed in "Eumaeus." The contrast between Parnell's polite behavior and John Henry Menton's piqued air after Bloom had assisted each of them with his hat gives rise to the notion of "history repeating itself with a difference" (*U* 535). Just as it was believed that "the prophets had full cognizance of all the incidents of the Incarnation, and were fully apprised of the Saviour's teaching and passion" (*Christian Doctrines* 68), Bloom and the text seem to possess a latent awareness of historical fulfillments.

But what I have expanded on primarily to this point is a two-pole system, when in fact a three-stage development takes place. A figure in the Old Testament may have been completed by its fulfillment in the New, but heavenly fulfillment was still forthcoming. Certain Christian writers, Augustine for one, emphasized three main steps: they perceived "the Law or history of the Jews as a prophetic *figura* for the appearance of Christ; the incarnation as fulfillment of this *figura* and at the same time as a new promise of the end of the world and the Last Judgment; and finally, the future occurrence of these events as ultimate fulfillment" ("Figura" 41).

This layout allows us to acknowledge the key role the apocalypse plays in typology, thus confirming my sense that Bloom's "Coming events cast their shadows before" is meant typologically, as it is surrounded by imagery of a general apocalyptic nature. The phrase "the ends of the world" occurs both before and after Bloom's remark, and Bloom at least puns on the Second Coming itself: considering the coincidences of the afternoon, he thinks, "*second* time. *Coming* events cast their shadows before" (*U* 135–36, my emphases). It does look as if the phrase "the ends of the world," whatever its literal meaning, is meant to refer to the apocalypse. Gifford and Seidman speculate that A.E.'s reference to "the twoheaded octopus, one of whose heads is the head upon which the ends of the world have forgotten to come" (*U* 135), may be to Macgregor Mathers, whose " 'two heads' were a . . . fanatic interest in what Yeats (*Autobiography*, p. 225) called 'the imminence of immense wars' (i.e., Armageddon, 'the ends of the world')" (*NJ* 139). And if "Coming events cast their shadows before" is from "Lochiel's Warning," a ballad by Thomas Campbell, this ballad itself concerns the imminence of an immense battle—a wizard predicts Bonnie Prince Charlie's defeat at Culloden and Lochiel's death in the fighting— and the wizard's foreknowledge is expressed in the language of apocalypse. The wizard's warning refers explicitly to the revelation of events known all along by God: "Lochiel, Lochiel, beware of day! / For, dark and despairing my sight I may seal, / But man cannot cover what God would reveal: / 'Tis the sunset of life gives me mystical lore, / And coming events cast their shadows before" (*NJ* 139).

This three-stage conception—the Old Testament fulfilled in the New, and the New Testament unfulfilled until the millennium—underlines the point that in horizontal typology a type and its antitype "have something provisional and incomplete about them; they point to . . . something in the future, something still to come, which will be the actual, real, and definitive event" ("Figura" 58). Put another way, history is "forever a figure, cloaked [as Auerbach says] and needful of interpretation" ("Figura" 58). The gap between event and event—between anticipation and satisfaction—is identified with the gap between act and interpretation: the antitype *is* the interpretation "promised and not yet present" ("Figura" 59). A process of deferral is, then, built into the figural system. The final moment of referentiality is postponed, as types point to antitypes that in turn become types, though truth is expected ultimately to come.

Let us presume to take God's point of view. That is, one way of facilitating our comprehension of horizontal typology as a kind of indirect vertical typology is to consider Tertullian's idea "that for God there is no *differentia temporis*" ("Figura" 42). Or we might entertain Augustine's reasoning that if God is omniscient, things "are not future to Him but present"; and therefore His knowledge should "be termed not foreknowledge, but simply knowledge" ("Figura" 43). There is a pressure within the historicity of typology pushing us to realize these transhistorical implications of God's omniscience. D. W. Robertson explains Augustine's sense that figurative expression urges us toward God: the "peculiar configuration" of the materials of figurative expression gives rise "to an abstract pattern which is coherent. The incoherence of the surface materials is almost essential to the formation of the abstract pattern, for if the surface materials—the concrete elements in the figure—were consistent or spontaneously satisfying in an emotional way, there would be no stimulus to seek something beyond them." Augustine (writes Robertson) felt that "a figurative expression offers an opportunity to discern the *invisibilia Dei* through 'the things that are made,' and [Augustine went even further] it has the effect of stimulating love for the *invisibilia.*"[9] Typology is a narrative that cannot look like a narrative: its divine coherence depends upon gaps, disruptions, mundane inconsequence.

Joyce was completely, obsessively, caught up in this typological network. In the same "incoherent," "inconsistent" way that biblical typology uncovers God's grand scheme, Joyce's own quirky secular typological structures intensify our awareness of his godlike control. Stephen's voluptuous dream, to take by way of introduction one example among hundreds, of a "street of harlots" and a man who leads him, holding a melon against his face (*U* 39), as it prefigures and is fulfilled by Bloom's guidance of Stephen in Nighttown as well as Bloom's offer to Stephen to view Molly's photograph, illustrates the process. Molly's picture fulfills Stephen's dream as it gives "a liberal display of bosom" (*U* 533); and if it is doubted that melons are meant to serve as a metaphoric synecdoche of Molly, in "Ithaca" we learn that before dropping off to sleep, Bloom kisses the "melons of her rump" (*U* 604). In this case we are offered blatant clues that guide our attention to Joyce's meddling hand, clutching his masterful pen: an authorial intrusion in "Scylla and Charybdis" (another is at the end of "Proteus" [*U* 39]) coaxes us to observe the eventual realization of Stephen's dream. Reflecting on his dream, Stephen thinks: "Last night I flew. Easily flew. Men wondered. Street of harlots after. A creamfruit melon he held to me." Then looms up, enigmatically, the sentence: "You will see" (*U* 179). It is as if Joyce intrudes here to alert us to the principle well illustrated in *Ulysses* that "Coming events cast their shadows before." Since "You will see" seems to spring from a consciousness that has knowledge of the future, as Stephen's cannot, these words compel the reader to acknowledge the artist-god who has organized and therefore comprehends the entire labyrinth (as God knows the world) at once.[10] (Yet the literal must not be abandoned: figural realism depends on it. It is likely that, on this level, "In. You will see" [*U* 217] is what the man holding a "creamfruit melon," tempting Stephen, whispers to Stephen to lure him: "[Come/Go] In. You will see [what/whom] I am leading you to [a woman who will really excite you]."[11] Earlier fragments from the dream strengthen this interpretation, but the line obviously need not be restricted to the literal.)

The idea of restriction, in fact, almost seems to contradict the spirit of typological exegesis. We might think of the Bible as being plural in that every type has a literal and spiritual referent, and possibly even multiple referents; and the more type and antitype combinations the interpreter discerns, the more impressive the testimony to God's plan. The pool of possibilities seems unbounded. One might even imagine typological exegetes "at play" with the texts of the Old and New Testaments, actively collaborating with the writers, and thus lessening the gap between the writing and reading processes: reading for them constituted the writing. One might theorize that the Bible was in this way produced rather than passively consumed.

And so we can begin to get a glimpse of how a novel modeled on biblical figural realism could turn gracefully from being Ricoeur's text to being Barthes's Text, in that some of the seeds of the Barthesian Text may be found in biblical hermeneutics. Barthes himself discerns these links. In *Criticism and Truth*, under the heading "Plural language," he takes up Ricoeur's idea of the symbol, which (in Ricoeur's words) "exists when language produces signs of a compound order where the meaning, not content to designate something, designates another meaning which could not be reached except by and through what is intended by it." Barthes then traces his appropriation of Ricoeur's symbol to the famous fourfold reading of the Bible. "The freedom of the symbol was recognized and to some extent encoded in the Middle Ages, as can be seen in the theory of the four meanings."[12] Reversing this direction, that is, using a contemporary reading to get back to medieval hermeneutics, one enterprising (producing, not consuming) critic of *Ulysses*, Hugh Kenner, locates so many idiosyncratic links between the first and second halves of the novel (for instance, "The letters of *Yes*, the last word, run backwards through *Stately*, the first") that he identifies as "a governing rhythm of the book" the process "whereby impression in the first half is modified by knowledge in the second, though only after resolute rereading has extracted the knowledge from a stylistic that tends to render it inconspicuous."[13] The affinity between Kenner's description and typology seems glaring.

My argument builds to this homology: while in the vertical register of typology earthly things are fulfilled ultimately in God's spiritual plan, the stuff of *Ulysses* is "fulfilled" in Joyce's linguistic plan. Just as vertical typology points from mundane events up to God, Joyce's fictional version of vertical typology points from the material world of *Ulysses* "up" to Joyce (as in the example of the figure and fulfillment of Stephen's voluptuous dream). And once we locate Joyce in his writing— once Joyce is conflated with his linguistic scheme—these two correspondences become synonymous.

Hence yet another Christian father-figure looms over Joyce's construction of *Ulysses*, as the ghostly presence of father/Father figures hovers over Joyce's every authorial move. The writer prior to Joyce who most fully represents the anagogic realm to which all figurae finally refer is Dante in the *Divine Comedy*. Instead of prefiguring spiritual events (the more common practice in figural realism), "The *Comedy* [writes Auerbach] is a vision which regards and proclaims the figural truth as already fulfilled" ("Figura" 67). Auerbach defends this conception of the *Divine Comedy* through his reading of three of its dominant characters—Cato, Virgil, and Beatrice. The earthly Cato "who renounced his life for freedom" serves as a figura of the Cato who appears in the *Purgatorio* as the "revealed or fulfilled figure." "The political and earthly freedom for which [Cato] died" is seen as an "*umbra futurorum:* a prefiguration of the Christian freedom whose guardian he is . . . appointed" in the *Purgatorio* ("Figura" 65–66). "The historical Virgil is 'fulfilled' by the dweller in limbo" ("Figura" 69). And Beatrice is both an actual woman from Dante's experience on earth and an "incarnation of revelation" ("Figura" 74–75). Like Cato and Virgil, Beatrice has a historical/spiritual twofold nature. However—and this is the tricky point—vertical typology is as concerned with history as is horizontal typology, the difference being simply that on the horizontal level both figure and fulfillment are originally earthly and historical events, whereas vertically the heavenly fulfillment incorporates the earthliness and historicity of the figure. It is precisely because the final divine order itself was believed to be concrete reality that Dante chose to express a vision of the beyond as a tangible place.

The pertinence to *Ulysses* of the *Divine Comedy* interpreted, as Auerbach interprets it, as a representation of *fulfilled* figurae (earthly and otherworldly at the same time) becomes apparent once we recognize—to take the first step—that in *Ulysses* signifiers with referents also parade their status as signifiers, and so divide the text into realistic and suprarealistic layers. The "coolwrappered soap" Bloom carries in his left hand in "Lotus-Eaters" (*U* 70) simultaneously signifies a real bar of soap in a real wrapper and exists as a novel, opaque, irreducible phrase. ("THE SOAP" asserts its vitality as language by returning in "Circe" as a character [*U* 360].) "Bloom" on one hand starts as a Dublin Jew, living at 7 Eccles Street, married to Molly, etc.; on the other "Bloom" becomes a word with its own potency, capable of generating related word-chains such as "Henry Flower." In the *Divine Comedy*—analogically, anagogically—Cato, Virgil, and Beatrice are historical figures even as they are inhabitants of the world beyond. To take the

second step: all the writing of *Ulysses*, by virtue of its irre-
ducibility, is ipso facto materially present, just as the spiritual
world in Dante is envisioned as a tangible place.

In tracing Joyce's modern adaptation of figural realism, one
must beware of getting buried in the details. And yet, it is
crucial to keep in mind—precisely while one is immersed in
such details—the peculiar relationship to his punishing past
that Joyce was working out. His identification with the patriarchal writers of figural realism, like his identification with
the fathers/Fathers in general, is half the story. His literary
imitation testifies that he knew he was one of them—in *both*
his realism and figural realism—but the baroque extreme to
which he takes that imitation suggests a strenuous effort to
release such patriarchal clamps. (Joyce's realistic detail eventually plunges to "prodigal detail," perhaps "feminine detail,"
resistant to "the fold of meaning" [Schor 85].) In writing about
Joyce and Dante, early on in his new biography, Richard Ellmann nicely captures this doubleness, bringing out curiously
the punitive streak in at least one of Joyce's literary forefathers:
"Dante was perhaps Joyce's favorite author, and Joyce was
as local and as scrupulous in vision; but he put aside Dante's
heaven and hell, sin and punishment," relishing "secular, disorderly lives which Dante would have punished or ignored"
(Ellmann 4). Divine vision founded on cruelty was to Joyce
an impossibility.

II

Ut implerentur scripturae
—Ulysses

Joyce's appropriated typology eventually achieves the status
of parody and splinters into wordplay. But this process is slow-
going and at first only borders on parody (at times Joyce even

appears to improve upon the layout of typological patterns in the Bible). His typological analogues suggest his attraction to biblical hermeneutics (his inability to give it up or get it off his mind), while they simultaneously function as sabotage. Joyce's strategy is duplicitous: he brings typology to an excessive level that bespeaks his utter complicity in the reading practices of the Church Fathers at the same time that such excessiveness and the meticulous as well as facetious nature of his literary cooptation prove to be ultimately reductive, even destructive.

It is not that every reference in *Ulysses* to the Old Testament occurs before "Sirens," or that every reference to the New Testament follows "Wandering Rocks" (a division to be justified later). Joyce was, predictably, not perfectly systematic in this way. Biblical allusions to both Testaments creep in insidiously everywhere. An ostensibly secular line in "Wandering Rocks"—"Boyd? Martin Cunningham said shortly. Touch me not" (*U* 202)—mimics Christ. "Touch me not; for I am not yet ascended to my Father" was Jesus' command to Mary Magdalene after the Resurrection (John 20:17). Still, fairly frequent predictions of the coming of Elijah as well as the conflation of both Stephen and Bloom with Moses in the novel's first part mark it as Joyce's secularized Old Testament. (Joyce's parallactic cloud alone identifies both Bloom and Stephen as Moses figures. Immediately after Bloom walks under the cloud in "Calypso," his mind fills up with Old Testament thoughts about the captivity of the Jews [*U* 50]. And shortly after the cloud obscures the sun in "Telemachus," Mulligan calls to Stephen, "Dedalus, come down like a good mosey" [*U* 8–9].) The Transfiguration scene at the conclusion of "Cyclops," the conflation of Stephen and Bloom with Christ, and a dramatization of the Parousia and three secular apocalypses mark the second part as Joyce's New Testament. All of which establishes Joyce's duplicitous stance vis-à-vis biblical hermeneutics, indicating the foundation on which he bases his eventual textual explosion of typology. Even as Joyce's biblical analogues walk on the edge of parody—that is, they are mechanical, no more than parts of a superficial puzzle the reader is led to assemble, a game the reader is intellectually seduced into—and thus move toward a kind of apocalyptic blowing up, they impress upon us his deep investment in the knowledge his Jesuit masters drilled into him.

Just as both Stephen and Bloom masquerade redundantly as Moses, they masquerade redundantly as Christ. In "Nestor," a popular image of Christ invades Stephen's mind: while teaching he thinks "of him that walked the waves." This image triggers thoughts of the various unworthy people over whom Christ's shadow lies, for example the Pharisees who offered Christ "a coin of the tribute"; Stephen's meditations on the Pharisees in turn lead him to quote mentally a part of Christ's enigmatic rebuttal to them: "To Caesar what is Caesar's, to God what is God's" (*U* 22). At the end of "Proteus," no such buildup to identification is necessary; Stephen thinks automatically in the words of Christ: "Come. I thirst" (*U* 42), a phrase that is typologically rich. Christ uttered it just before dying on the cross, "knowing that all things were now accomplished, that the scripture might be fulfilled" (John 19:28). It is Stephen's namesake, St. Stephen, who in his Defense tells of Moses' prediction to the children of Israel: "A Prophet shall the Lord your God raise up unto you of your brethren, like unto me; him shall ye hear" (Acts 7:37); the prophet seems at moments to be Stephen himself, already likened to Moses.

The oddity—since nothing would have been easier than to attach Moses to Bloom as precursor of Christ as suffering Stephen—is that Joyce endows Bloom as well with Christ's words. In "sticking in an odd word" in "Cyclops"—"Some people, says Bloom, can see the mote in others' eyes but they can't see the beam in their own" (*U* 267)—Bloom paraphrases Christ, who preaches at the end of the Sermon on the Mount, "And why beholdest thou the mote that is in thy brother's

eye, but considerest not the beam that is in thine own eye?"
(Matt. 7:3). Stephen testifies directly to Bloom's identity as
Christ: in "Eumaeus," he mumbles, "*Christus* or Bloom his
name is" (*U* 525). And in "Lestrygonians," in at first incor-
rectly reading a throwaway, Bloom names himself Christ:
"Bloo. . . . Me? No. Blood of the Lamb" (*U* 124). In the mes-
sianic scene in "Circe," in which Bloom announces the "*new
Bloomusalem*" (*U* 395), the self-identification is more asser-
tive: when "A VOICE" in "Circe" asks Bloom, "Are you the
Messiah ben Joseph or ben David?" Bloom replies, "You have
said it" (*U* 403–04), echoing Jesus' answer, "Thou sayest it,"
to Pilate's question, "Art thou the King of the Jews?" (Luke
23:3). Clothed in the garb Jesus wore at the crucifixion—"*a
seamless garment*"—Bloom finally expires in flames, uttering
an Irish version of Christ's words ("Daughters of Jerusalem,
weep not for me, but weep for yourselves, and for your children") to the women who "bewailed and lamented him" (Luke
23:27–28); Bloom's adaptation is "Weep not for me, O
daughters of Erin" (*U* 406).

It is easier to recite these examples than to classify them.
They are not serious yet just as certainly not negligible. Although some of Stephen's and Bloom's messianism is obviously
in their heads, Joyce cooperates with their typological self-
aggrandizement. As the typological parallels get more involved
and outrageous, the question may become whether Joyce is
revealing his own theological predilections. In as petty an act
as studying his nails in "Hades" (*U* 76), Bloom is likened to
Christ, especially since toward the end of "Lotus-Eaters" he
recalls Molly's interpretation of I.N.R.I.: "Iron nails ran in"
(*U* 66). Bloom's rapport with the bat overhead in "Nausicaa"
identifies him with Christ; in "Scylla and Charybdis," there
is an account of Christ "put upon by His fiends, stripped and
whipped . . . nailed like bat to barndoor" (*U* 162). In "Lestrygonians," the image of a "headless sardine" collapses the
two: "Under the sandwichbell lay on a bier of bread one last,

one lonely, last sardine of summer. Bloom alone" (*U* 237).
(Not only is the sardine a likely emblem of Christ because it
is a fish, but sardines are served at Stephen's Last Supper ceremony in "Oxen.") These thinner and more roundabout biblical links bring out the doubleness of Joyce's relation to his
patristic precursors, indicating a fuller investment and identification on the one hand, and an attenuation of biblical significance on the other, as the parallels begin to seem prepos-
terous. The Christ-Bloom parallel finally becomes part of a
paronomastic nexus by means of Joyce's play on "Eumaeus"/
Emmaus (where Jesus made a special appeal to His disciples
to understand Him through events of the Old Testament):
Bloom's "nocturnal perambulation to and from the cabman's
shelter" (*U* 599) parallels "Jesus' 'Walk to Emmaus,' His first
appearance after the resurrection."[14]

Joyce, then, dramatizes playfully—at once mystifying and
demystifying—Old and New Dispensations as Stephen and
Bloom don the dual masks of Moses and Christ. Just as Moses
prefigures Christ and Christ becomes the New Moses by fulfilling the Law, both Stephen and Bloom, by surpassing their
roles as Moses figures, by in a sense fulfilling in one role what
they promise in another, enact the same pattern, linking the
two halves, the Old and New Testaments, so to speak, of
Ulysses. Joyce avoids an allegorical one-to-one correspondence
between Moses and Bloom, and Christ and Stephen—or, for
that matter, between Moses and Stephen, and Christ and
Bloom—which compels us to find an interpretative strategy
by which Moses and Christ are identified. As the author of
both halves of his own Bible and its typological exegete at
once, Joyce can improve upon the identification of Moses and
Christ: he can *plant* Christ in Moses, and Moses in Christ.
This is as if doing a service for the typological hermeneutics
of the Church Fathers; but it also brings out the absurdity of
the enterprise.[15]

Joyce had the further advantage of being able to supply the

apocalyptic fulfillment of his own figural history. Whereas the
Bible has to be content to predict a future congruent with
prior events, *Ulysses* collapses all the times of typology, giving
a sense, however ludicrously, of divine simultaneity. Not only
phase one (the history of the Jews prefigured events of the
New Testament) and phase two (the Incarnation fulfilled the
Old Testament and promised the end of the world and final
judgment) but the third phase of typology (the chance of salvation brought about by the Incarnation "pointed believers
to certain great eschatological events located in the future"
[*Christian Doctrines* 459]) appears (as in Dante) in *Ulysses*.
Joyce presents his version of the Parousia (Bloom as the returned Christ brings about "the *new Bloomusalem*" [*U* 395])
and three versions of the catastrophic ending of the world:
as noted in "Ithaca," "the disorderly house of Mrs Bella Cohen, 82 Tyrone street" becomes the site of "Armaggedon" (*U*
599).

An apocalyptic fire burns at the end of "Oxen." Something
is ablaze (the text reads "Blaze on" [*U* 349]); a bit later Bloom
refers to a "Big blaze" on the South side (*U* 355); and the fire
brigade (as signaled by the repeated word "Pflaap!" [*U* 349,
406]) appears to be speedily on the way. Amidst the hodge-
podge of linguistic fragments that concludes "Oxen," an explicit reference to the Judgment surfaces that makes us see in
this local fire the final holocaust: "Even now that day is at
hand when he shall come to judge the world by fire" (*U* 349).
We know that Joyce is considering the end of the world here
antitypically, since what follows is the Latin *"Ut implerentur
scripturae"* ("That the scriptures might be fulfilled").[16]

Joyce's second and third renditions of the apocalypse, both
in "Circe," are less merely allusive. Florry announces "The
end of the world!"—represented as *"a twoheaded octopus in
gillie's kilts, busby and tartan filibegs"* (*U* 413)—and then
"THE END OF THE WORLD" takes form as a "Circean"
character and speaks: *"(with a Scotch accent)* Wha'll dance

the keel row, the keel row, the kell row?" (*U* 414). This conception of course springs from A.E.'s earlier remarks, which Bloom overhears in "Lestrygonians," on "the twoheaded octopus, one of whose heads is the head upon which the ends of the world have forgotten to come while the other speaks with a Scotch accent" (*U* 135). Sandwiched between this thought of A.E.'s and a related but shorter one of Bloom's, "The ends of the world with a Scotch accent" (*U* 136), we recall, is Bloom's "Coming events cast their shadows before" (*U* 135). This definition of typology, then, not only gains its religious force through apocalyptic references between which it lies, but it turns out to pertain to "THE END OF THE WORLD" in "Circe," a coming event whose shadow it itself casts before in "Lestrygonians."

Joyce fills in his history of Revelation with the sexual high jinks of Bella and Bloom, as they seem meant to parallel the goings-on between the Whore of Babylon and the beast: whore-mistress Bella (as "Bello") rides Bloom (*U* 435) just as "BABYLON THE GREAT" straddles the beast (Rev. 17:3–5). "ALEXANDER J. DOWIE," speaking in "Circe," confirms the parallel by calling Bloom "a worshipper of the Scarlet Woman" (*U* 401). Completing the eschatological picture is Joyce's third apocalypse near the close of "Circe." The event begins as "DISTANT VOICES" cry, "Dublin's burning! Dublin's burning! On fire, on fire!" *"Pandemonium"* breaks loose; *"The earth trembles";* there are myriad catastrophic activities (*U* 488–89). "THE VOICE OF ALL THE DAMNED" and "THE VOICE OF ALL THE BLESSED" (*U* 489) appear, now eternally divided.

I have arranged the typological analogues presented here for the most part by moving from the less to the more frivolous, though probably every illustration invoked has some humor lurking behind it. Yet typological hermeneutics is serious business in the sense that what is at stake is the justification of a God who seems to change His mind and needs history to take a new direction, without making Him seem whimsical or willful. That Joyce makes light of the process is epitomized in the following double entendre: at the beginning of one of the apocalyptic scenes in "Circe," *"A rocket rushes up the sky and bursts. A white star falls from it, proclaiming the consummation of all things and second coming of Elijah"* (*U* 413). But how does a rocket signify the "second coming of Elijah"? By association with the "Roman candle" of "Nausicaa" (*U* 300) (which, juxtaposed with Bloom's onanism in that chapter, is clearly a sexual metaphor), this rocket too must have sexual connotations. Thus in "Nausicaa" is the first, in "Circe" the second, coming. The subversiveness of Joyce's literary biblical analogues (as it has been threatening to do all along) rears its ugly head. Joyce's tedious labyrinthine commitment to biblical hermeneutics is reinvested in linguistic play, in this case in a dirty joke. He teases it and teases it and in the process teases us into missing his gradual and thus insidious sabotage, until something nasty appears.

Joyce clinches the joke by spreading over "Aeolus" a giant pun on "type," signifying both newspaper print and biblical figures and events. Bold type serves as the medium for a title that features Moses, "VIRGILIAN, SAYS PEDAGOGUE. SOPHOMORE PLUMPS FOR OLD MAN MOSES". (*U* 122), for two titles reminiscent of Christ, "THE WEARER OF THE CROWN" (*U* 96) and "SUFFICIENT FOR THE DAY . . ." (*U* 114) (a phrase from Jesus' Sermon on the Mount [Matt. 6:34]), and for a title, "FROM THE FATHERS," that refers to early typologists, the Church Fathers (the first line of this column quotes St. Augustine) (*U* 117).

The news blurb entitled "AND IT WAS THE FEAST OF THE PASSOVER" draws attention to itself as type (being in bold print) while referring to a holiday—Passover—that celebrates a major Old Testament event read by the Church Fathers as a type prefiguring Christ. Within this news report,

Bloom's observation of, and subsequent observations on, the process of printing lead directly to his meditation on typological occurrences in the Old Testament. The point of transition from typography to typology is Bloom's perception that set type is "backwards": "He stayed in his walk to watch a typesetter neatly distributing type. Reads it backwards first. Quickly he does it. Must require some practice that. mangiD. kcirtaP. Poor papa with his hagadah book, reading backwards with his finger to me" (*U* 101). Set type, specifically "mangiD. kcirtaP" ("Patrick Dignam" backward), catalyzes Bloom's thoughts on his father's Haggadah, since the Haggadah Hebrew is read from right to left.

Once Bloom fixes on the Haggadah, he spins out a series of thoughts on Old Testament events foreshadowing their fulfillments: "Pessach. Next year in Jerusalem. Dear, O dear! All that long business about that brought us out of the land of Egypt and into the house of bondage [a Bloomian variation on the theme] *alleluia. Shema Israel Adonai Elohenu . . .*" (*U 101). By pondering the phrase* "Next year in Jerusalem," which "climaxes a prayer to God to 'rebuild . . . Jerusalem, the city of holiness' " (*NJ* 105), and by subsequently alluding to the angel of death, whose own death, according to the words of the Haggadah, "marks the day when the kingdom of the Almighty will be established on earth" and "Israel will live in perfect redemption in the promised land" (*NJ* 105), Bloom evokes the idea of the New Jerusalem, an ultimate antitype. Then his mind slips with ease from types back to typography, from concentrating on the Jewish exodus to noticing the typesetter in front of him: "Sounds a bit silly till you come to look into it well. Justice it means but it's everybody eating everyone else. That's what life is after all. How quickly he does that job. Practice makes perfect. Seems to see with his fingers" (*U* 101). The typology/typography pun is thus raveled and unraveled.

III

Like the final chapter of a Victorian novel, "Ithaca"
abounds in detailed revelations that refocus what we had
thought we knew and substantiate what we only
guessed.
  In doing this it restresses a governing rhythm of the
book, whereby impression in the first half is modified by
knowledge in the second, though only after resolute re-
reading has extracted the knowledge from a stylistic that
tends to render it inconspicuous.
—Hugh Kenner, *Ulysses*

Joyce's fetishization of typology, that is, his translation of it
into sheer literary and linguistic ornament, begins gradually
to crystallize. He went to even more extravagant lengths than
I have intimated. Michael Groden points out in *Ulysses in*
Progress that while Joyce was writing the later episodes of
Ulysses, he was "accumulating additions for the completed
episodes." As late as July 12, 1920, Joyce told Harriet Weaver
that "he had brought to Paris 'an extract of insertions for the
first half of the book.' " According to Groden, "occasionally
Joyce introduced a phrase into a late episode and simultaneously planted preparations for it in earlier ones." Groden's
most vivid examples of this process are Joyce's inclusion of
"the phrase 'the Parable of the Plums' as Stephen's subtitle
for his 'Pisgah Sight of Palestine' in the Rosenbach copybook
of 'Ithaca' . . . at about the same time that he was adding it
to 'Aeolus' " and his addition of "a stylistic preparation for
Gerty MacDowell's episode in the summer of 1921 when he
inserted a phrase in her idiom into the last section of 'Wandering Rocks.' "[17]
  This method of building up *Ulysses* inscribes a typological
pattern (of which, considering the explicit and pervasive use
Joyce made of traditional types and antitypes, I would assume
he was perfectly aware) that ultimately gives to typology a

purely linguistic status. As Kenner and others have been on the verge of noticing,[18] Joyce tended to think typologically, in terms of realistic events that gain suprarealistic meaning when looked at retrospectively as predictions; this was, loosely speaking, a kind of epistemological necessity for him (conscious or not). Two, sometimes inextricable, formal strategies in *Ulysses* appear to be modeled on typology: a typology of the plot—whereby an action or object in the first part foreshadows and is somehow completed by an action or object in the second part—and a typology of language.

In the former case, it must be emphasized that it is not that an event occurs and then simply recurs; the repetition is not a typological repetition unless new meaning is conferred upon the first event by the second. Yet, although the first event gains significance from, or is perhaps rounded off by, the second, it at the same time retains its original significance. This pattern of prefiguration and fulfillment is ingrained in the basic fabric—the narrative or story line—of *Ulysses*. It is traceable, for example, in the relationship of Bloom's memory in "Lestrygonians" of himself making love to Molly on Howth one sunny afternoon sixteen years ago (*U* 144) and its typological fulfillment in the blissful closing lines of the book. Molly and Bloom reconstruct the scene through many of the same images: rhododendrons, the sun, sea, sky, seedcake, luscious kissing, and Molly's breasts. It is natural that they conjure up some of the same images; but that they invoke almost exactly the same images, one after another, Bloom in the former and Molly in the latter half of the novel, suggests a typological configuration. And upon reading Molly's memory, we apprehend the incompleteness of Bloom's. Her reminiscence, unlike his, includes the vital added fact of Bloom's proposal of marriage. Thanks to Molly's memory, Bloom's, seemingly complete at the time, is seen retrospectively, when it is fulfilled, as incomplete—as needing the conclusive retelling it finally undergoes.

What Bloom's story lacks is its *consummation*—Bloom's various failures to consummate and Molly's craving for consummation are paradigmatic of the typological structure on the narrative level. In "Calypso," Molly poses a question to Bloom about *Ruby: the Pride of the Ring*—"Is she in love with the first fellow all the time?" (*U* 53)—which is no doubt meant to reflect on the outcome of the plot of *Ulysses*. Since Bloom appears customarily to pick up Molly's pulp fiction, and therefore in all probability has at least skimmed *Ruby*, Molly's question is realistic enough. Yet our subsequent knowledge of the events of *Ulysses* gives the inquiry a retrospective interest quite beyond our curiosity about Molly's or Bloom's interpretation of the romantic action of the pulp novel.

Bloom's shopping for a replacement of *Ruby* in "Wandering Rocks" results in the exposure of another sentimental plot designed obviously, in an even more elaborate and poignant way, to parallel his own circumstances on June 16, 1904. Not even the first-time reader peruses the excerpts from *Sweets of Sin* without aligning the heroine—with her *"opulent curves,"* her *"queenly shoulders and heaving embonpoint"* (*U* 194)— with Molly, her cuckolded husband with Bloom, and Raoul with Boylan. It is no doubt masochistic Bloom's own sense of these correlations that prompts him to purchase the book. (Kenner regards Bloom's act of bringing *Sweets of Sin* home to Molly as his way of ensuring that she knows "that he apprehends the analogy," a detail that is to Kenner "one of the pluckiest and saddest . . . this rich book has to offer.")[19] As if to vindicate our sense that the adulterous plot of *Sweets of Sin* has been fulfilled by the adulterous plot of the novel, Joyce collapses Molly with the pulp novel heroine. Her photograph and *Sweets of Sin* are juxtaposed, literally, in Bloom's pocket. Reaching into his pocket, Bloom avoids *Sweets of Sin* to take out Molly's photo; but given the way Molly's picture is described, we may wonder if the pulp heroine has been left behind. "[T]he slightly soiled photo [is] creased by opulent curves," and Bloom glances off in order not to increase Stephen's "possible embarrassment while gauging her symmetry of heaving *embonpoint*" (*U* 533–34).

  Bloom's absorption with the ad for Plumtree's potted meat again prefigures Molly's consummation. While conducting a superficial conversation with M'Coy in "Lotus-Eaters," Bloom catches a glimpse of the ad in the newspaper he (Bloom) is carrying:

> *What is home without*
> *Plumtree's Potted Meat?*
>   *Incomplete.*
> *With it an abode of bliss.* [*U* 61]

Later, appropriately in the food-filled universe of "Lestrygonians," Bloom recalls the ad and denounces it: "Potted meats. What is home without Plumtree's potted meat? Incomplete. What a stupid ad!" (*U* 140). The peculiarity is that Molly and Boylan, in the initial stages of their dalliance, indulge in this product. Having returned home, Bloom finds in the kitchen dresser, among the leftovers of Molly and Boylan's afternoon party, "an empty pot of Plumtree's potted meat" (*U* 552). It is doubtful that there is a causal link (as there never is in typological connections) between Molly and Boylan's consumption of potted meat and Bloom's early preoccupation with the ad; even if Bloom's attention is drawn to it because (in a moment of unconscious crudity) he associates potted meat with Molly, it is still improbable that he could have anticipated that Molly and Boylan would share a pot of it that afternoon. Bloom's anxiety over the ad, nonetheless, presages and is fulfilled by the alimentary ritual Molly and Boylan perform before turning Bloom into a cuckold. After we read about the empty pot, both Bloom's fixation on and subsequent criticism of the advertisement have an import they previously lacked; we understand at this point why Joyce has made the desirability of a home with Plumtree's potted meat disquieting to Bloom. Joyce's joke works happily on both typological and sexual levels: Bloom's irritation lies in the fact that the incomplete is completed and therefore brings about a "heavenly" "abode of bliss."

In divesting typology of its theological high seriousness, Joyce is fetishizing it—which is in a way an appropriate thing to do to it, a kind of critique by doubling, as typology is, like fetishism, a fixation on making what is incomplete, complete. Thus we can see in Joyce's deliberate fetishizing a sympathy with Bloom's *position:* though doubling Blazes's *place* in the heavenly abode of bliss, Bloom takes himself out of position to effect a heavenly consummation. The "fat pears" that comprise part of Boylan's gift of a fruit basket to Molly, as they lie "head by tail" (*U* 187), predict the positions of Molly and Bloom in bed at the end of the novel. The pears, because of their "head by tail" position, become significant prefiguratively once we read late in the book about Molly and Bloom's sleeping arrangement—Molly, "S.E. by E."; Bloom, "N.W. by W." (*U* 606)—and so may be said to be postfigured by the couple's habitual alignment.

It is no coincidence that the most outstanding instances of narrative typology in *Ulysses* focus on the Bloom marriage (its ups and downs) and end with the question of consummation—Molly with Bloom, and Molly with Boylan—since the union of type and antitype itself *is* a consummation. That is, Joyce adds the standard bawdy pun to Christ's *"Consummatum est,"* itself, as Stephen Greenblatt points out, a delicate play on the typological tag, *"ut consummaretur Scriptura."*[20] Perhaps Joyce is also extending his joke on the "first" and "second coming," or perhaps he is playing with the typological link between Adam (father of [sexual] sin) and Jesus, as Boylan turns Molly into Eve and Bloom turns her into Mary (by avoiding consummation). Joyce's pun on "heavenly abode of bliss" might then connote Eden, where Molly/Eve sins with

Boylan/Adam. And the two consummations in the novel, one in time (Molly's union with Boylan) and one out of time (Molly's memory, placed later in the book, of her union with Bloom), allow a final Paradise to mimic the first one sixteen years ago, with the sin in the middle. These are typological games Joyce may or may not be playing. The more serious proposal I would make is that Joyce moves typology, the reading strategy of the Church Fathers, toward its limit by moving it in the direction of Molly.

He pushes typology in the direction of language as well, which parallel movement certainly begins to allow us to glimpse a connection between language and the *femina vita* to which Joyce perceived the Church as hostile. Stephen's scribbling on his Mosaic "table of rock" (*U* 40) by the sea in "Proteus" catalyzes a transitional instance, since writing is folded into the action itself. Stephen's urge to write at the beach prefigures Bloom's desire in "Nausicaa" to do the same. Though what Stephen writes is not unveiled to us, we do learn Bloom's message: "I. . . . AM. A" (*U* 312); and perhaps Stephen's subsequent thought "As I am. As I am" (*U* 41) is meant as a clue to the complete meaning of Bloom's unfinished sentence. There are religious—more specifically, biblical, even typological—overtones to the events of these two scenes. Stephen's scribbling on a "table of rock" aligns him with Moses; Bloom's "I. . . . AM. A" imitates the beginning of "I am Alpha and Omega" in Revelation (Rev. 1:8 and 11; 21:6 and 22:13). Bloom's message also echoes the beginning of God's words to Moses, "I AM THAT I AM" (Exodus 3:14); if Stephen's phrase "As I am. As I am" is taken as an indication of how Bloom's is meant to end, and Bloom has in mind the full message "I am as I am," then Bloom's partly unstated message almost duplicates God's statement of his identity to Moses.

Bloom answers indirectly the question Stephen poses about his writing in "Proteus": "Who ever anywhere will read these written words?" (*U* 40). After effacing the letters he has

scratched in the sand, Bloom "replies": "All fades" (*U* 312).
As an antitype fulfills a type, Bloom's statement on the transience of writing seems to have been made in response to, and
therefore may be said to complete, Stephen's speculations on
the subject—with an amusing irony. The fact of Bloom's reply
negates his message that "all fades"; Stephen's question has
survived at some level. This irony bears its own relevance to
typology: since typology unveils an eternal plan, it is necessarily the contradiction of transience. An event occurs (perhaps, as in this case, a self-consciously ephemeral event) that
is followed by another. Yet in the repetition of the two
ephemeral events is the timeless pattern.

Writing is the common denominator of these two scenes.
Prior to scribbling on the rock, Stephen reminds himself that
he is in possession of "Old Deasy's letter" (*U* 40). Bloom turns
over in his mind phrases from Martha Clifford's letter, in between printing letters (in another sense of the word) in the
sand, and conceives of his sand writing as "a message for
[Gerty]" (*U* 312). While Stephen asks himself, "What is that
word known to all men?" (*U* 41), Bloom, thinking in a parallel
construction (and punning on Martha's slip of the pen), wonders, "What is the meaning of that other world?" (*U* 312).
Even more remarkable than this is the use *Stephen* seems to
make of Martha's mistake. Thinking on (at least) two levels
at once about stars and words, Stephen ponders, "Darkly they
are there behind this light, darkness shining in the brightness,
delta of Cassiopeia, worlds" (*U* 40). He employs "worlds"
fittingly to refer to the astronomical realms he is considering,
but a pun on "words" is also germane: the phrase "darkness
shining in the brightness" actually makes more sense as a description of words than of stars. This is corroborated by Stephen's conception of his words written on the rock as "signs
on a white field," and a moment later he has the mysterious
thought "You find my words dark" (*U* 40). The oddity is that
at this point the world/word pun is being alluded to before

it has come into being. It is established in Martha Clifford's letter—"I called you naughty boy because I do not like that other world. Please tell me what is the real meaning of that word" (*U* 63)—and its status as a full-fledged pun is secure by the time Bloom uses it in "Nausicaa." Here then is an antitype functioning perfectly: until the scene in "Nausicaa," we cannot grasp the widest possible reverberations of the scene in "Proteus"; we possess all the facts but are unable to read them fully, in all their rich complexity, until they are postfigured.

Joyce's linguistic typological repetitions, like his narrative typology, adhere to the two rudimentary criteria of typological hermeneutics: that the antitype cast a new light on the type, and that the type (in spite of this illumination) retain its original meaning. As Joyce gives typology a purely linguistic form, however, it resembles decreasingly its theological model. Its weight lessens; it lightens. Joyce empties out this hermeneutical practice of his Fathers (as he liberates himself from their clutches) through eventually reducing their strategy for reading the Bible to an organizing principle of word games. But we will work up to Joyce's more capricious recasting of typology; as always Joyce roots his parody in the real thing.

The full significance of Stephen's vaguely apocalyptic words in the Telemachiad (they derive from passages in Blake wherein the apocalypse is the explicit subject [*NJ* 20]) is not unveiled until we read about Stephen's climactic shattering of the chandelier in "Circe." Stephen's Blakean meditations first surface in "Nestor": "Fabled by the daughters of memory. And yet it was in some way if not as memory fabled it. A phrase, then, of impatience, thud of Blake's wings of excess. I hear the ruin of all space, shattered glass and toppling masonry, and time one livid final flame. What's left us then?" (*U* 20). In "Proteus," there is some duplication: "Shattered glass and toppling masonry" (*U* 36) resurfaces in Stephen's mind. In "Circe," the linguistic antitype appears. These same words revive to describe Stephen's act of violence in the brothel: *"He lifts his ashplant high with both hands and smashes the chandelier. Time's livid final flame leaps and, in the following darkness, ruin of all space, shattered glass and toppling masonry"* (U 475). The appropriateness of applying Stephen's earlier apocalyptic language to this act of local destruction is confirmed in that the action occurs directly after "THE MOTHER" refers to her "anguish when expiring with love, grief and agony on Mount Calvary" (U 475), making Stephen's subsequent role that of Christ in the apocalypse, and in that it exists in the novel's most apocalyptic episode. In the light of the antitype, the earlier fragmented versions of it emerge as predictions; Stephen's vague eschatological thoughts have been realized. One answer to his question "What's left us then?" is to find for (Blakean) prophetic words their (Joycean) material counterparts. It becomes evident why early on Stephen shapes thoughts in language he does not quite approve of; his original thoughts—even though thudding in the spirit of Blake's excess—turn out to be necessary, *ut implerentur scripturae.*

The typological spirit may linger merely in the overtones of incantatory phrases; take, for example, the relation of the prefigurative word "rosewood" and its postfiguration, "rose upon the rood of time." Stephen invokes the term "rosewood" in the Telemachiad to describe the odor of his mother when she appears to him in a dream: "Silently, in a dream she had come to him after her death, her wasted body within its loose brown graveclothes giving off an odour of wax and rosewood, her breath, that had bent upon him, mute, reproachful, a faint odour of wetted ashes" (U 5). The same morbid lyricism is repeated a bit later, but this time the arrangement of words has changed, new words having been added, some elided: "In a dream, silently, she had come to him, her wasted body within its loose graveclothes giving off an odour of wax and rosewood, her breath bent over him with mute secret words, a

faint odour of wetted ashes" (*U* 9). The repetition and alter-
ation signal the linguistic antitype. Joyce calls attention to
some of the most prominent of these words by giving them
yet a third avatar: "She was no more: the trembling skeleton
of a twig burnt in the fire, an odour of rosewood and wetted
ashes" (*U* 23). And upon reading much later a transmutation
of the word "rosewood," we run up against religious implications. In his postcreation speech in "Oxen," Stephen splits
"rosewood" in half, replaces "wood" with a more particular
sense of the word—"rood"—and uses it again. "Desire's wind
blasts the thorntree but after it becomes from a bramblebush
to be a rose upon the rood of time" (*U* 320).

Besides alluding to the dedicatory poem, "The Rose Upon
the Rood of Time," of Yeats's *The Rose,* Stephen is reciting
a homily of St. Bernard of Clairvaux, which is "included in
the *Divine Office* for 7 October, the Feast of the Blessed Virgin
Mary of the Rosary." The homily contrasts Eve, "a thorn
fastening death upon all," with Mary, "a rose giving the heritage of salvation back to all" (*NJ* 341–42), and so brings
typology to bear directly—since Eve pretypifies Mary (Stephen
himself labels her "the second Eve" [*U* 320])—on the meaning
of Stephen's words in "Oxen," and retrospectively on their
prefiguration, the repeated word "rosewood." Once we have
acknowledged that at least one function of "rose upon the
rood of time" is to contrast Mary with Eve, we may wish to
return to the context of the earlier convergence of "rose" and
"wood" to hunt for traces of the mother not of life but of
death. Our search is rewarded in Stephen's images of his own
mother, as they underscore her mortal nature, and the mortality she seems to exhale: her body is "wasted," her graveclothes musty; her breath, redolent of ashes, seems to breathe
death rather than life into Stephen.

Eve's death is not merely a prefiguration of Mary's life: death
itself is a consummation ("*Consummatum est*"), and May
Dedalus is its prophet. In "Proteus," Stephen ponders "the

handmaid of the moon" in beautifully modulated terms: "Bridebed, childbed, bed of death, ghostcandled. *Omnis caro ad te veniet*" (*U* 40). From here his thoughts continue to flow lyrically from sea to morbid sexual imagery, via the image of a "pale vampire," whose "bat sails" bloody the sea, and who ends up pressing his "mouth to her mouth's kiss" (*U* 40). Then follows Stephen's notorious conflation of womb with tomb—"His lips lipped and mouthed fleshless lips of air: mouth to her moomb. Oomb, allwombing tomb" (*U* 40)— bringing us back full circle to the sea, the "bed of death," as Stephen initially labels it. Stephen's Latin may therefore be interpreted to mean that all flesh will eventually return to the sea as the symbolic locus of death. And as Stephen accepts in the Telemachiad Mulligan's designation, born in the spirit of Swinburne, of the sea as "a great sweet mother" (*U* 5), we may wish to invoke May Dedalus as a Swinburnean mother of oceanic proportions, her enormous womb a tomb finally capable of embracing everything. We have then this metonymic chain: the sea, death, the mother's womb/tomb.

But when the Latin phrase *"Omnis caro ad te veniet"* emerges for a second time, it follows on the heels of Stephen's postcreation speech, which, though it first invokes mortality—in a phrase reminiscent of the earlier passage, "In woman's womb word is made flesh"—evolves to show the means of transcending mortality, "but in the spirit of the maker all flesh that passes becomes the word that shall not pass away. This is the postcreation. *Omnis caro ad te veniet*" (*U* 320). The "thee" to which all flesh will return, in this case, appears to be art; Stephen theorizes that the "maker" or artist arrests permanently "all flesh that passes," transforming it, presumably in literary art, to "the word that shall not pass away." Seen in the light of the latter *"Omnis caro ad te veniet,"* the former looms as an expression of the antithesis to the artistic process. Just as "rosewood" prefigures "rose upon the rood of time," though its connotations are antithetical to it, just as Eve as the mother of death prefigures Mary as the mother of life, here the early idea of flesh returning to the sea, to death, to the mortal mother's womb serves as an ironic prefiguration of the later definition of art—as a "womb of the imagination"[21]—in the postcreation speech. Joyce repudiates the real mother's womb, while he worships it in its imaginary form; in fact, it is where Molly emerges as antitypical Mary, pregnant with the final word of *Ulysses,* as opposed to her typical incarnation as Eve with Blazes (we will see), that all the historical events of *Ulysses* are recast as a tour de force of linguistic imagination.

By now the duplicity of Joyce's strategy (and consequently of my argument) must be apparent. His literary appropriation of typology builds up the analogy between *Ulysses* and the Bible. For one thing Joyce's adaptation of biblical hermeneutics depends heavily on biblical material. For another, to reverse the chronology, his adaptation brings out the Joycean maze-like structure of the Bible itself—Frye describes the Bible as a "mosaic: a pattern of commandments, aphorisms, epigrams, proverbs, parables, riddles, pericopes, parallel couplets, for-mulaic phrases, folktales, oracles, epiphanies, *Gattungen, Logia,* bits of occasional verse, marginal glosses, legends, snippets from historical documents, laws, letters, sermons, hymns, ec-static visions, rituals, fables, genealogical lists, and so on al-most indefinitely," as "a miscellaneous mass of material," a "vast labyrinth," whose typological relations he sorts out.[22] Joyce's typology underscores the movement in *Ulysses* from world to word, a progression that reproduces the Bible's (1) realistic, historical Old Testament and (2) less realistic, less historical, more spiritual, Word-centered New Testament structure. Joyce expands Martha Clifford's world/word pun to the parameters of the novel itself, since from the point of view of the "wordy half" of the book, one can return to the more "worldly half" (as poststructuralist critics have done) to witness the word in the world, a conflation (Word/world) absolutely central in biblical typology.

But—and herein lurks the duplicity I speak of—Joyce's parodic exhaustion of the typological process constitutes a further step, a fetishization of biblical hermeneutics whereby types and antitypes become empty shells. Joyce's linguistic typology roots out even more radically (than does his narrative typology) the possibility of stable meaning. By textualizing typology in this way, Joyce disassembles (this time on a grand scale) the typology/typography pun in "Aeolus." Typology diminishes to mere typography: typography casts off the heavy cloak of typology. Joyce seizes patriarchal hermeneutics for his own use, or rather, his own play. Yet he could not have turned it to pleasure without first working through it, so that any excess that Joyce may arrive at evolves directly out of patriarchal structures he was initially caught within.

The process generally begins with a word or phrase in the first part of *Ulysses* that has a clear referent; but when it crops up in the second part, its nonreferential status is privileged. The repetition of the word or phrase signals its metamorphosis from a transparency to an opacity, or perhaps I should say brings out its latent opacity. For as J. Hillis Miller asserts, "Any literary text is both self-referential and extra-referential, or rather it is open to being not seen as the former and mistakenly taken as the latter. All language is figurative, displaced. All language is beside itself."[23] Joyce writes in a way that keeps us from ignoring the "figurative," in Hillis Miller's sense of the word, nature of language; and (what is more striking) he arrives at his demonstration of the unending figurativeness of language via the vehicle of the figura. Joyce's network of typological figuration evolves into a free-floating signifying system, no longer content to remain under the restriction of a notion of final fulfillment.

"Auk's egg" fits the pattern paradigmatically. The phrase

first appears as a metaphor for the quaker librarian's head in "Scylla and Charybdis": "Felicitously he ceased and held a meek head among them, auk's egg, prize of their fray" (*U* 161). Gifford and Seidman offer two relevant facts: that the female auk's egg is "marbled and blotched with a variety of colors" (probably why it is used as an image of Mr. Lyster's head), and that if the "great auk" is being referred to, it is "a species but recently extinct in 1904" (*NJ* 179). As a means of describing Mr. Lyster's head, "auk's egg" works in the interest of realism, and since the great auk was an extant before it was an extinct bird, a referent may spring readily to mind when we read about its egg. But because the great auk had had its day by the time of *Ulysses,* there is a pressure in the phrase nudging us from the real to the unreal; if we are impervious to this pressure as we read "Scylla and Charybdis," at any rate, we certainly feel it as we reflect back on the phrase from the vantage point of its antitype. "Auk's egg" makes an appearance again, as is well known, at the end of "Ithaca," where the possessive noun "roc's" has been affixed to it: the egg is now a "roc's auk's egg" (*U* 607). If the auk's egg has become a possession of a roc, then it has become, at the very least, imaginary, for "the roc was a mythical bird of Arabia, so huge that it carried off elephants to feed its young" (*NJ* 494). But even one's imagination (not only one's reason) is defeated in trying to conceptualize the real product of the extinct product of an imaginary creature.

The defeat of imagination is felt most acutely when one notices that the unlikely egg is "square round": since geometry is an imaginary realm to begin with, and since the quadrature of the circle is impossible in it, we are compelled to realize that "square round" is not an imaginary formula but is purely verbal. What was once real but went extinct has been resurrected not by imagination but by language. At the end of "Ithaca," we have a pair of rhyming words—"roc's auk's"— that, peculiar as it sounds, possesses an egg. In the terms of

Joyce's literary typology, the linguistic type, "auk's egg," functioning realistically, prefigures and is fulfilled by its linguistic antitype, "roc's auk's egg," existing in its verbal self-containment, appropriately near the novel's end.

Joyce's elaboration of Auerbach's figural realism, then, sets in motion writing that enacts the figurative nature of language, in Hillis Miller's sense: "figural" splits off from realism. A type (signifier) refers to an antitype (signified) that in turn becomes a type (signifier), only now ad infinitum. Joyce reproduces but then unleashes the traditional three-part typological system as *Ulysses* expands into a Text. For once a word or phrase is released from the constraint of representation—which release by definition characterizes what I have called Joyce's linguistic antitypes—its signifying possibilities are unlimited.

At times, it is foregrounded that the disburdening of representational constraints is an antipatriarchal act. In "Nestor," Stephen defines God famously as "a shout in the street" (*U* 28), already shrinking Him in the linguistic type. His definition, we realize later, foreshadows a line in "Oxen": "A black crack of noise in the street here, alack, bawled back" (*U* 323). What is originally a prosaically expressed—if original—conception of God has become a rhyming, alliterating, staccato string of words (hence the linguistic antitype). Though the line in "Oxen" signifies thunder, its technical flourishes seize our attention. We read the line as onomatopoeia, in fact, almost on faith rather than because we hear something like the sound of thunder crackling through the words; in its context the line seduces us into thinking that it mimics the sound of thunder, but if merely a few of its words were modified, and the context were pastoralized, we could as easily hear in it the quacking of ducks.

Not only God but a ferocious God is turned into linguistic artifice: we are in the midst of an outburst of Thor's wrath. The style, aptly, has returned to mock Anglo-Saxon—witness the kenning and the exaggerated alliteration of "Loud on left Thor thundered: in anger awful the hammerhurler" (*U* 323). The onomatopoeia, like all onomatopoeia conventional to begin with, is specifically designed to appear to meet Old English conventions: no Latinisms, of course, and emphasized alliteration. Writing, verbal gymnastics, is on show. Stephen's rather flat "a shout in the street" has achieved a linguistic ontology in the eventual contrived and flamboyant technical display.

It was no doubt the illogical, antinarrative aspect of typology that rendered it amenable in the first place to the transformation into textuality that Joyce puts it through. In Frye's words "typological thinking is not rational thinking, and we have to get used to conceptions that do not follow ordinary distinctions of categories and are, so to speak, liquid rather than solid."[24] In harmony with this, the most fruitful place in *Ulysses* to locate Joyce's typology is in his literary equivalent to Revelation—his irrational "Circe." Michael Groden writes: "By the time [Joyce] finished 'Circe' he had included so much previous material that, in addition to the characters' psyches, *Ulysses* itself was turned inside-out."[25] Likewise, the writer of Revelation (according to Frye) "seems to have been closer to the Hebrew text of the Old Testament than most New Testament writers."[26]

By the end of "Circe," the cross-connections of language with itself stretch typology to its breaking point. Bello embellishes a cliché by using a rather eccentric phrase "secondbest bed"—"You have made your secondbest bed and others must lie in it" (*U* 443)—and in so doing repeats words prominent in a chapter, "Scylla and Charybdis," that she has nothing to do with. It is pertinent to Stephen's theory of Shakespeare that the poet left to Ann Hathaway (supposedly because of her infidelities) only, as Stephen says, a "secondbest bed" (*U* 169). If we entertain for a moment the possibility that Bello uses the phrase because Bloom has mentally foisted it on her (we have to rule out Stephen since he is not nearby), we must face the stumbling block that Bloom had left the room before "secondbest bed" gained prominence in "Scylla and Charybdis." As a linguistic type, "secondbest bed" plays a role in a critical theory; in Bella's mouth it verges on nonsense.

Non-sense—non-communication, figuration without reference—is precisely the point. In "Hades," on one of his usual mental rambles, Bloom thinks, "There are more women than men in the world" (*U* 84); in "Circe," we encounter this thought again only expressed, in almost the same words, by "THE MOTHER": "More women than men in the world," she instructs Stephen (*U* 473). Because Bloom is not in the proximity of "THE MOTHER" when she makes this statement, and Stephen is, and because she is Stephen's mother (she identifies herself as "May Goulding" [*U* 473]), it is feasible that she is Stephen's, not Bloom's, hallucination. But Bloom's mental peregrinations have prefigured hers; his thoughts have invaded her mind. Because, as Kenner writes, "Circe" is "an artifact that cannot be analyzed into any save literary constituents,"[27] it serves as a vast repository of antitypes that "elevate" their prefigurations to the status of textual events.

If in Christian typology a book is completed by a Man, as Harold Bloom puts it, in "Circean" typology, language is completed by language, and people seem to be merely language-effects. Leopold Bloom notices in "Lestrygonians" that "stuck on the pane two flies buzzed, stuck" (*U* 144); and in "Scylla and Charybdis," in the cryptic line "Buzz. Buzz" (*U* 156), the word qua word already seems to be asserting itself. Since the buzzing flies make an impression on Bloom in "Lestrygonians," "BROTHER BUZZ" in "Circe" may well be his concoction, but even if this is the case (especially since the word has metamorphosed into a character), it is as if "buzz" possesses the force to effect its own repetition. The role of skeptic that "BROTHER BUZZ" plays in "Circe" ("BUZZ" goads Bloom skeptically to "perform a miracle" [*U* 404], and later dresses him to be sacrificed by fire [*U* 406]) bears little relation to the word's previous connotation in "Lestrygonians" of the sound of amorous flies. What might have been taken as an extension of Joyce's typology of words manifests a referential chain gone haywire. Links between all these buzz sounds and words may be initially discernible, thus invoking an artist-god who set them up; but with the "antitype" "BROTHER BUZZ," it becomes apparent that all referentiality is up for grabs—"buzz" explodes into significances beyond the typological network. There are no longer any limits on the word (purloined from *Hamlet*), which may at this point refer to or "do" anything.

By translating typology into a literary system and showing how that system may be entirely alienated from theology so that it becomes solely a structuring principle (the absurdity of "BROTHER BUZZ" as an antitype must not be lost sight of), Joyce fetishizes biblical hermeneutics. He fixes on "the shell instead of the substance," which is, perhaps ironically (given Joyce's rebellion), the way Puritans put their attack against Catholics, seeing them as fetishists or worshipers of external things.[28] Joyce's textualization of biblical hermeneutics gradually generates a linguistic system that insists that words are forever figures with unending capacity to refer to more figures, a movement built into but finally under control and terminated in typology. Through a rewriting of the biblical interpretative practices of his Fathers, strangely enough, Joyce achieves a ludic relationship to language, disseminating rather than mastering words, doing without, like Bloom, the expected consummations.

IV

He attempts to compose a discourse which is not uttered in the name of the Law and/or Violence: whose instance might be neither political nor religious nor scientific;

which might be in a sense the remainder and the supple-
ment of all such utterances. What shall we call such dis-
course? erotic, no doubt, for it has to do with pleasure;
or even perhaps: aesthetic, if we foresee subjecting this
old category to a gradual torsion which will alienate it
from its regressive, idealist background and bring it clos-
er to the body, to the drift.
—Roland Barthes, *Roland Barthes by Roland Barthes*

It is to the world of writing that the Sirens introduces
the reader.
—MacCabe, *James Joyce and the Revolution of the*
    Word

I have proposed that Joyce preserves patriarchy insofar as he
writes representationally but that the shift in *Ulysses* to a freer
play of the signifier reflects his subversion of the fathers/Fa-
thers. I have also argued that through his use of theology as
subject matter and structuring device, Joyce keeps alive the
Fathers, who in turn eventually become the primary target of
his retaliating pen, as theology plunges to textuality. Through
Joyce's adaptation of typology, we have seen a good deal of
the latter, that is, the breakdown of theological content; the
way Joyce escapes from the fathers/Fathers purely stylistically
needs elaboration.

  This can be done through further justification of splitting
Ulysses between "Wandering Rocks" and "Sirens" to de-
marcate the book's equivalents of Old and New Testaments,
since the general metamorphosis from representation to self-
referentiality thereby becomes vivid. It may be that ultimately
(the adverb is my contribution to MacCabe's sentence) "*Ulys-*
ses and *Finnegans Wake* are concerned not with representing
experience through language but with experiencing language
through a destruction of representation" and that in Joyce's
texts "all positions are constantly threatened with dissolution

into the play of language" (MacCabe 4, 14), but Joyce needed
to set up the illusion of full presence before he could do, or
seem to do, away with it. (I am not sure he ever relinquished
this illusion; it may simply change form, from the deceptive
fullness of naturalism to the illusion of synecdochic plenitude.)
The first "half" of *Ulysses,* at least, bears more of a kinship
with classical realism than MacCabe acknowledges. Patron-
izing the fathers/Fathers, Joyce initially produces writing that
strains to establish (phallogocentrically) one-to-one correspondences between word and thing.

One of Hugh Kenner's famous discoveries is that the first
two pages of *A Portrait* are "an Aristotelian catalogue of senses."[29] The first page of "Calypso" outdoes even the beginning
of *A Portrait* in Aristotelian concrete sensuousness. As we enter
Bloom's kitchen, sense impressions cannot help but overlap.
Although the main feature of the scene is food, not only taste
but the other senses as well are invoked. The opening paragraph is principally a list of dishes prepared with "the inner
organs of beasts and fowls" (*U* 45) and thus makes its most
direct appeal to taste; yet the adjective "thick" in "thick giblet
soup" piques our sense of touch, and the "fine tang of faintly
scented urine" that kidneys bring to Bloom's palate stimulates
our olfactory sense. Paragraph two arouses primarily the sense
of touch: Bloom moves about the kitchen "softly"; he rights
the objects on Molly's "humpy" tray; the air and light outside
are "gelid"; it is a "gentle summer morning." We next encounter coals "reddening" and are further invited to visualize
the kettle, sitting on the hob: "dull and squat, its spout stuck
out." There is an appeal to both our senses of touch and sight
in Joyce's description of the coals and kettle, as in his description of Bloom's cat: from the "reddening" coals, we get
a tactile datum—heat—by means of a visual one—color; the
adjective "dull" conveys the texture of the kettle as well as
its appearance; and the "sleek hide" of Bloom's cat suggests
both slipperiness and shininess. Joyce gives things tactile as

well as visual allure by dwelling on their textures. Joyce employs detail, even heavily sensuous detail, that poses no threat but instead gives rise to the illusion of organic wholeness. There are no insignificant details, hence no extravagant details. Striving for representational fullness, without linguistic excess, Joyce exhibits his masterful virtuosity.

Just as his fathers/Fathers were compelled to master the victims of their various punishing rods, Joyce was compelled initially to master reality with his pen. Mimesis here surpasses its usual limits, words often performing double duty to render as much representational detail as possible. Joyce adopts the position of quintessential realist; his gesture is phallic in the sense that the "Calypso" scene denies any "absence on which it is constructed . . . and assert[s] reality as the presence which provides the text with a simple origin outside language" (MacCabe 95–96). But as Joyce piles up detail after detail, the potential arises for a diminution, a disruption, rather than an enhancement of realism. (These processes are interdependent; he would and could not have been involved in one without the other.) The threat to organic wholeness averted earlier now surfaces. From a "systematic, totalizing aesthetics" (Hegel's aesthetics, as Schor explains), *Ulysses* shifts to one that is "detotalized and fragmentary" (Barthes's aesthetics). The insignificant, inessential detail is privileged, which, as Schor writes, is "tantamount to attacking the foundation of hermeneutics . . . constantly engaged in shuttling between the part and the whole" (Schor 80, 85).

The part, in and of itself, takes over, as for example in "Ithaca," where we find ourselves in the same cluttered kitchen, being asked to notice the same dull, squat kettle. Invoking a parallel to the "Calypso" scene, the catechizer of this section queries, "What did Bloom do at the range?" This question leads to a comparatively terse, straightforward answer comprised of detail (though mechanically given) similar to what we have just witnessed: "He removed the saucepan to the left hob, rose and carried the iron kettle to the sink in order to tap the current by turning the faucet to let it flow" (*U* 548). But with the answer to the following question—"Did it flow?"—we are thrust into excessive detail that overwhelms our ability to continue attaching particular words to mental pictures, and that thereby disrupts the whole realist picture:

> Yes. From Roundwood reservoir in county Wicklow of a cubic capacity of 2400 million gallons, percolating through a subterranean aqueduct of filter mains of single and double pipeage constructed at an initial plant cost of £5 per linear yard by way of the Dargle, Rathdown, Glen of the Downs and Callowhill to the 26 acre reservoir at Stillorgan, a distance of 22 statute miles, and thence, through a system of relieving tanks, by a gradient of 250 feet to the city boundary at Eustace bridge, upper Leeson street, though from prolonged summer drouth and daily supply of 12 1/2 million gallons the water had fallen below the sill of the overflow weir for which reason the borough surveyor and waterworks engineer, Mr Spencer Harty, C. E., on the instructions of the waterworks committee had prohibited the use of municipal water for purposes other than those of consumption (envisaging the possibility of recourse being had to the impotable water of the Grand and Royal canals as in 1893) particularly as the South Dublin Guardians, notwithstanding their ration of 15 gallons per day per pauper supplied through a 6 inch meter, had been convicted of a wastage of 20,000 gallons per night by a reading of their meter on the affirmation of the law agent of the corporation, Mr Ignatius Rice, solicitor, thereby acting to the detriment of another section of the public, selfsupporting taxpayers, solvent, sound. [*U* 548]

Representation collapses. Because we cannot process this passage (and even begin to lose track of early facts we might have processed), we instead become immersed in an order of language. (Mr. Spencer Harty or Mr. Ignatius Rice might have been any invented name in this world of apparent hyperfactuality.) Joyce explodes the earlier delusion of (phallic) full presence; stylistic excess supersedes narrative. Like the Barthesian detail, the Joycean detail becomes "supplementary, marginal, decentered," and fetishistically appealing (Schor 91).

Joyce's lists—perhaps the most referential possible language, typically nouns in an apparently easy relationship to reality— illustrate this same usurpation, as realism yields to an irreducible network of writing, to useless textual detail. In general, "Sirens" signals the change. Probably the part of *Ulysses* before "Sirens" that best resembles the lists of "Cyclops" (and so would afford the fairest comparison) is the last section of "Wandering Rocks" (*U* 207–09). Enumerated here are the names of much of the cast of *Ulysses*. Although Stephen and Bloom are conspicuously absent and Gerty (since she has not yet made her debut in the story) is conspicuously present, still it is—with the exception perhaps of the river Poddle, "Henry, *dernier cri* James," and Marie Kendall, the girl on the poster— a list of conventional items. Almost every name recorded refers to a person in the book; no two names are welded together (like "Gould Lidwell" and "Pat Bloom" in "Sirens" [*U* 226] or *"Bloombella Kittylynch Florryzoe"* in "Circe" [*U* 472]); and though there is some alliteration, and "socks" is set up to rhyme with "clocks," wordplay does not predominate.

Any of the catalogues of names in "Cyclops" furnishes a useful contrast. Hanging from our Irish hero's girdle is a row of seastones on which are carved "the tribal images of many Irish heroes and heroines of antiquity" (*U* 244), but the list of names that follows is hardly confined to "Irish heroes and heroines of antiquity." Ancient Irish heroes and heroines do turn up, but the list soon reveals its capacity to embrace anything: "The Woman Who Didn't," "Patrick W. Shakespeare," "Dolly Mount" (*U* 244). We find an assortment of names from history, myth, fiction, as well as from the realm of nonsense, and are forced to acknowledge that the only world in which, say, Dante Alighieri and Adam and Eve can consort with the Bride of Lammermoor and the Rose of Castile is a literary one. It is probably no accident that with his playful pen Joyce in this way sabotages the hero—epitome of masculinity—just as in this same chapter he parodies "the phenomenon which has been denominated by the faculty a morbid upwards and outwards philoprogenitive erection *in articulo mortis per diminutionem capitis*" (*U* 250). It is a dead man— here the hanged man—who has phallic potency; Joyce would seem to prefer Bloom's feminized member—"the limp father of thousands, a languid floating flower" (*U* 71). All of which might lead one to wonder, as Schor does throughout *Reading in Detail:* "Is the [excessive] detail feminine?" (Schor 97).

Like Joyce's lists, letters before "Sirens" and after "Wandering Rocks" record the translation from work to text, from full presence (or its illusion) to linguistic play, and analogously from Old to New Testament. While Joyce's lists stress the caving in of a typically referential (and therefore resistant) form to textuality, the novel's letters—being inherently self-reflexive in their presentation (and not representation) of words—swing in the direction of textuality. Both Milly's and Martha's letters to Bloom (*U* 54, 63–64), though riddled with bad grammar, poor sentence structure, childish, inexact diction, and the choppiness of short, declarative sentences, are not self-subversive. But Bloom's reply to Martha in "Sirens" is, comparatively speaking, a muddle.

> Dear Henry wrote: dear Mady. Got your lett and flow. Hell did I put? Some pock or oth. It is utterl imposs. Underline *imposs*. To write today.
>   Bore this. Bored Bloom tambourined gently with I am just reflecting fingers on flat pad Pat brought.
>   On. Know what I mean. No, change that ee. Accep my poor litt pres enclos. Ask her no answ. Hold on. Five Dig.

Two about here. Penny the gulls. Elijah is com. Seven Davy
Byrne's. Is eight about. Say half a crown. My poor little
pres: p. o. two and six. Write me a long. Do you despise?
Jingle, have you the? So excited. Why do you call me
naught? You naughty too? O, Mairy lost the string of her.
Bye for today. Yes, yes, will tell you. Want to. To keep it
up. Call me that other. Other world she wrote. My patience
are exhaust. To keep it up. You must believe. Believe. The
tank. It. Is. True. [*U* 229]

Bloom's letter must be unraveled from the surrounding text,
though the point is that it cannot be, as language reverts to
language. Whereas Milly's and Martha's letters are differ-
entiated from the surrounding text, fragments of Bloom's in-
cipient letter (for example, "Why do you call me naught?"—
which transforms the expected "naughty" to its literal meaning
"nothing") are strung together with Bloom's thoughts of the
moment ("My patience are exhaust"), along with fragments
we have encountered previously and tend to regard as textual
motifs ("Elijah is com" and "Jingle"), though they may inhabit
Bloom's mind as well. Bloom's postscript closes the question
of writing as subject. He lops off the potential sentence, "How
will you punish me?" so that it reads, "How will you pun?"
(*U* 230)—an unmistakable allusion to the process at hand.
   Apparently in a hurry, Bloom uses idiosyncratic abbreviations
pervasively ("lett" for letter, "flow" for flower); his sentences
too sometimes go unfinished ("Write me a long"). Not only
are these truncations eye-catching, but they lead us astray,
generating a network of signifiers that have little to do with
Bloom's epistolary intentions. They drift. "Lett" and "flow"
in this liquid novel of association might easily glide into "let
flow" or "menstrual flow"; and "Write me a long," in sound-
ing like "Write me along," may for a second call up phrases
such as "Take me along" or "String me along." Bloom's
shorthand teases us to toy with his words, to fiddle with his

meanings. Joyce may intend here a revelation of Bloom's unconscious; or he may be employing a punning (purely textual and not psychological) way of demonstrating that *Ulysses* evolves into a literary equivalent not to heroism but to "languid floating flower[s]."

Everything prior to "Sirens" (perhaps especially "Proteus") is by no means perfectly lucid, unentangled, or realistic. Joyce's representational work is forever being ruptured before then, though more quietly. Yet there is nothing in the first part like the "fifty-eight linguistic fragments," to revive Kenner's label, that launch "Sirens."[30] Besides repetitions of itself, "Sirens" also heavily interweaves material from all the earlier chapters. Frye describes one of the most striking features of the Bible as its ability to regenerate itself, and it is now a truism that *Ulysses* self-recreates. In "Sirens," the regeneration often is explicitly a matter of language: repetition of an event or thing alone would have suggested such regeneration, but the point of textual reproduction is intensified by the replication of linguistic action. George Lidwell's question "What are the wild waves saying?" (*U* 231) seems provoked not only by the "fourworded wavespeech" in "Proteus" (*U* 41) but by "Wavewhite wedded words shimmering on the dim tide" in "Telemachus" (*U* 8). "Calypso" contributes part of its famous first line to "Sirens," as the text self-consciously asserts: "Pat served, uncovered dishes. Leopold cut liverslices. As said before he ate with relish the inner organs, nutty gizzards, fried cods' roes" (*U* 221). Bloom remembers Molly's trouble with "metempsychosis" (*U* 52) in his Mollyesque thought "Met him pike hoses. Philosophy. O rocks!" (*U* 234). The main bond between "Lotus-Eaters" and "Sirens" is the correspondence of Martha's letter (*U* 63–64) with Bloom's reply (*U* 229). The Fetter Lane passages from Stephen's Shakespeare theory join "Scylla and Charybdis" and "Sirens." And the viceregal cavalcade that moves through "Wandering Rocks" generates the motif that begins "Sirens"—"Bronze by gold heard the hoof-

irons, steelyringing. Imperthnthn thnthnthn" (*U* 210). The first
"bronze by gold" variation appears in "Wandering Rocks":
"Above the crossblind of the Ormond Hotel, gold by bronze,
Miss Kennedy's head by Miss Douce's head watched and ad-
mired" (*U* 207). "Sirens" is so heavily laden with the irrepressible writing from earlier chapters that one is prompted
to quote Bloom: "Coming events cast their shadows before."
The book's evolution from representation to linguistic tapestry
again follows a buried typological pattern, dividing "Old"
from "New Testament." Of course, it may already be sus-
pected that the self-recreation of the Bible that begins at
the Gospels must be fundamentally different from the self-
recreation of *Ulysses* at "Sirens": the Good News for all Mankind must be antithetical to the bad news for men that the
Sirens offer (the promise of eternal life antithetical to the
promise of sudden death). Another way to put this might be
that where the Bible self-recreates, *Ulysses* self-deconstructs.
Where the Church Fathers impose unity on history and text,
the Sirens allow an infinite expression of textuality: line-
arity, like the heroes of the *Odyssey,* is devastated. With
the Sirens' help, Penelope's tapestry begins to loom large.

"Sirens" not only stylistically marks the slide in *Ulysses* from
realism to linguistic play (from the "masculine" to the "feminine" detail), but the story it tells indicts phallic power. The
"singing" Bloom hears throughout this episode interlaces allusions to Boylan's "proud knocker with a cock carracarra-
carra cock. Cockcock" (*U* 232) (which reduces to "Cockcar-
racarra" [*U* 233] and variations on it) with the "Tap" of the
blind stripling's cane: "With a cock with a carra. / Tap. Tap.
Tap" (*U* 235). Male potency is mingled with impotency, suggesting (as in *Dubliners* through the collapsing of castrating
fathers with castrated sons) a bond between the two: Dublin
men who flaunt their virility only reveal their attempts at
compensation. Even more reminiscent of *Dubliners* is that
while the blind piano tuner carries a cane, Boylan gets linked

metonymically with a whip. "By Bachelor's walk jogjaunty jingled Blazes Boylan, bachelor, in sun in heat, mare's glossy rump atrot, with flick of whip, on bounding tyres: sprawled, warmseated, Boylan impatience, ardentbold. Horn. Have you the? Horn. Have you the? Haw haw horn" (*U* 222). To have the "horn" is to be laughed at in "Sirens." It is tantamount to possessing a beerpull: "On the smooth jutting beerpull laid Lydia hand, light, plumply, leave it to my hands. . . . Fro, to: to, fro: over the polished knob . . ." (*U* 235). Joyce continues this assault on machismo in "Circe," where Bello praises Boylan's "weapon with knobs and lumps and warts all over it" (*U* 441). Perhaps the only major character who lacks interiority, Blazes Boylan comes forward as mere/pure phallic energy. Through his exposé of this brute in "Sirens," Joyce thematizes the novel's shift to a nonphallic style—a siren's song, a flow not a thrust, a "Flood of warm jamjam lickitup secretness [that] flowed to flow in music out, in desire, dark to lick flow invading" (*U* 226).

V

> *The author is reputed the father and owner of his*
> *work. . . . As for the Text, it reads without the inscrip-*
> *tion of the Father. . . . [T]he metaphor of the Text is that*
> *of the network. . . . [I]t can be read without the guaran-*
> *tee of its father. . . . It is not that the Author may not*
> *"come back" in the Text. . . . [H]is inscription is ludic.*
> —Barthes, *Image Music Text*

Compelled by his attachment to his patriarchal past, Joyce, I have argued, imitates the Church Fathers by producing a book modeled on biblical typology; but the idiosyncratic, extravagant parodic style of his imitation enables him to shake himself loose from them, even to spin out from figural realism a dramatization of the figurative nature of language, which in turn challenges the Father's signature. Joyce's cooptation of typology, his emptying of the logic of ful-fillment, in the end moves *Ulysses* to the status of a Barthesian Text. But while evolving typologically, *Ulysses* offers Joyce the chance to adopt the role of Creator-God, a patriarchal position of supreme (literary) power and control, most appropriate to one whose preference for the pen grew out of a difficult rejection of the whip. (In metaphoric sexual terms, until "Sirens" Joyce-as-writer may be said to follow Blazes Boylan, before he comes to repudiate him, in himself.)

In imitation of the God of Tertullian, for whom "there is no *differentia temporis,*" Joyce constructed *Ulysses* (in a way his pointedly chronological novel) achronologically. The insertions Groden reveals to have been injected into already completed chapters testify to Joyce's achronological method. But *Ulysses* was not only constructed achronologically—it is an achronological construction. The appropriation of elements of the first part (despite the timing of their insertion) by the second part indicates a consciousness above the particular elements, ordering them in a way that implies the passage of time, but whose very act of so ordering them requires a comprehension of them all at once. The Bible, the novel's prototype, appears to proceed through time, from B.C. to A.D., but events of the Old and New Testaments, like the figures Moses and Christ, exist to God in one eternal moment. Analogically, though the majority of readers experience *Ulysses* by proceeding from the first part to the second, encountering Stephen and Bloom as Moses figures before encountering them as Christ figures, meeting secular types before recognizing their antitypes, for Joyce, overseeing omnisciently the vast pattern from his artist-god pedestal, everything that constitutes *Ulysses* exists simultaneously as part of one elaborate plan.

Many Joyce critics (even feminist critics) have been willing to grant to Joyce this kind of power over his writing. In her afterword to *Women in Joyce,* Carolyn Heilbrun writes glowingly:

The claims of James Joyce upon immortality are unique and multiple. Chief among these is our consciousness of his effort and achievement. No critic, however industrious . . . has been able to discover in Joyce's writings anything which Joyce did not, with deliberation, put there. In anticipating the ideal insomniac as his reader, Joyce must have delighted in the knowledge that, however complicated the processes to be uncovered in his work, no one would reveal anything which exceeded or betrayed his intention. There are no more accidents in *Ulysses* than in the Parthenon: all is planned. Unconscious ambiguity is as unknown to Joyce as it is palpable in all his great contemporaries."[31]

No doubt Heilbrun means to praise Joyce through this homage to his mastery. But verbal mastery (Joyce's literary pandybat), though he certainly possessed it and therefore I suppose invited his readers to laud him for it, was something Joyce was cursed with, something he would have sooner dispossessed. His overall treatment of typology suggests that instead of maintaining the role of Master, he sets loose the chain of figures and fulfillments (which in the orthodox system finally refer to God) to the point that they no longer refer "up" to him but seem self-propelled. The figural system traditionally closed by God is pried open by Joyce, thus enabling Joyce critics to generate unending commentary and in doing so to reveal, as Attridge and Ferrer write,

> the infinite productivity of interpretative activity, the impossibility of closing off the processes of signification, the incessant shifting and opening-out of meaning in the act of reading and re-reading. The dream of final and total explication seems to be turning into a prospect of interminable accumulation—which can be experienced as a Borgesian nightmare of inescapable repetition or a Rabelaisian vision of infinite and comic fecundity. There is no doubt which view Joyce would have taken.[32]

The varieties of criticism themselves—one stressing Joyce's mastery, the other infinite interpretative possibilities—would indicate a battle in *Ulysses* between authorial control and a textual overthrow of that control. Even some of the most sophisticated statements of the primacy of textuality in Joyce's writing reveal the underlying typological pattern out of which infinite linguistic productivity finally breaks through. Attridge and Ferrer assert that "the endeavour is not to assimilate *Finnegans Wake* and the last chapters of *Ulysses* to the traditional elements present in the early works but to look at this apparently traditional writing in the light of the most radical aspects of the later texts."[33] Is not this poststructuralist strategy a matter of "light" because in Joyce "Coming events cast their shadows before"?

3

Rose Upon
the Rood
of Time

I

Has her roses probably.
—Leopold Bloom, *Ulysses*

From theology to textuality, to textuality via theology—
this is a constitutive move of *Ulysses*. What appears at
first glance to be a tribute to the Fathers evolves into a
means of casting them off. Joyce, in Derrida's terms,
"borrows from a heritage the resources necessary for the
deconstruction of that heritage itself."[1] But Joyce is as
obsessive about what he constructs as he is about the
process of dismantling that construction.

  His literary demystification of the Mystery of the Eucharist follows this format. Joyce weaves the Eucharist
intricately into his narrative. The sacrament frames the
book, since in a sense *Ulysses* begins with Buck Mulligan's communion service and ends as Molly and Bloom
confect their own private eucharist ("Moist with spittle
[Ellmann writes], the seedcake offers its parallel also to
the host")[2] Sandwiched between these two "eucharists"
are official Catholic Eucharists, as well as a profusion

73

of secular eucharists—from Stephen and Bloom's early morning snack of cocoa to, say, Professor MacHugh's nibbling on a "water biscuit," if the idea that so minor an act is justifiably considered to be eucharistic may be swallowed for the moment. I think that it should be, but there is a turning point at which Joyce's secularizing begins to look like fetishization, a valorizing of the outer sign rather than the inner substance. Joyce's antic multiplication of eucharistic images leads gradually to a shriveling, a drying up of the original theological significance. The Eucharist ends up providing Joyce with a linguistic paradigm that, as in the case of typology, results in the dissolution of the initially preserved theology.

In *A Portrait,* Cranly interrogates Stephen on the subject of taking communion: "And is that why you will not communicate . . . because you feel that the host . . . may be the body and blood of the son of God and not a wafer of bread? And because you fear that it may be?" Stephen affirms this, adding: "I imagine . . . that there is a malevolent reality behind those things I say I fear." To Cranly's question of why Stephen refuses to make "a sacrilegious communion," Stephen shapes a literary (even punning) answer: "I fear . . . the chemical action which would be set up in my soul by a false homage to a symbol behind which are massed twenty centuries of authority and veneration" (P 243). As in all the scenes of whipping rehearsed earlier, here again patrilineal tyranny asserts itself, this time twenty centuries of religious authority, twenty centuries of the malevolent reality of the Fathers—all packed into a dreadful symbol. What Joyce would have to do then to abolish that authority's power over him, to relieve himself of his dread of it, was disassemble the sacrament. And so he translates the Eucharist into secular form and overdoes the bread/body and wine/blood imagery. As Fritz Senn would articulate it, Joyce gets "carried away" with Eucharistic/eucharistic provection, to the point that the analogy collapses under its own weight.

Eucharist, or bread/body and wine/blood, imagery is virtually ubiquitous in *Ulysses*.[3] References to Catholic Eucharistic services are sprinkled throughout the book. (Stephen imagines in "Proteus" "a priest round the corner . . . elevating [the host]. Dringdring! And two streets off another locking it into a pyx. Dringadring!" [*U* 33]. Father Conmee in "Wandering Rocks" raises "his hat to the Blessed Sacrament" [*U* 182] and is later described as standing "at the altarrails [placing] the host with difficulty in the mouth of the awkward old man who had the shaky head" [*U* 183]. Bloom observes in "Lotus-Eaters" the communion ritual, makes erroneous comments about it, and remarks on its cannibalistic nature [*U* 66]. And the benediction of the "Most Blessed Sacrament" forms a dominant motif in the middle of "Nausicaa.") Suggesting the centrality of the Eucharist to Joyce's imagination, simultaneously with his aim to win the Mystery from the Church and his desire to mock it, *Ulysses* overflows with secular eucharists. Stephen and Bloom's imbibing in "Ithaca" of "Epps's massproduct, the creature cocoa" (*U* 553) has been famously sacramentalized, along with the coffee and bun that Stephen and Bloom sit down to in "Eumaeus" (*U* 509), as well as Bloom's bathing body as he consecrates himself with the appropriate words—"This is my body"—in his tub-chalice in "Lotus-Eaters" (*U* 71), as well as Gerty MacDowell herself, as well as (the list goes on) Bloom's lunch in "Lestrygonians"—"Wine soaked and softened rolled pith of bread . . ." (*U* 143).[4] The list is, and I think is designed to be, exhausting.

If fetishism is, as David Simpson in *Fetishism and Imagination* defines it, the worshiping of the symbol over the thing symbolized, then, to return momentarily to Stephen in *A Portrait,* there is fetishism implicit in Stephen's fearful regard for the Eucharist insofar as he dreads its symbolic power—its longevity and highly venerated abstract force—rather than its reality as the body and blood of Christ. Stephen seems to repeat an error "central to the ancient religions" in believing that "the sign, the figure, or the symbol had the same force, the same supernatural power, and the same benevolent or protecting faculties as those which were attributed to the sacred object thus figured or symbolized; that the sign was worth as much as the thing signified."[5] Joyce's secularization of the Eucharist in a sense perpetuates this same "misunderstanding," or perhaps I should say that Joyce "misunderstands" more egregiously, and certainly more deliberately, than Stephen, since in *A Portrait* the Eucharist is taken to be real and symbolic, while in *Ulysses* it becomes a symbol that is emptied so as to revert to its accidents. Images of bread and blood in *Ulysses*, especially as they are repeated with a vengeance, lose their affiliation with, and eventually acquire more weight within the novel than, the religious Mystery that justified and inspired their existence in the first place. But if Stephen's fetishization of the host, his devotion to it as a kind of unreal presence, nourishes his fear, Joyce's provides a means of conquering it.

If we follow a few of the astounding number of Dubliners in *Ulysses* who are preparing to eat, are in the process of eating, or have just eaten "our staple food," as Bloom labels it, then both the broad expansion of Joyce's secularization of the Eucharist and its concomitant diminution of theological meaning become clear. As in the case of Joyce's typology, the more widely the doctrine proliferates, ironically the more subversive his doctrinal gesture. Even secular Bloom cannot eat ordinary bread without its transubstantiating into an analogue of the host. Prior to purchasing "two Banbury cakes for a penny," he reads the words "Blood of the Lamb" on Dowie's throwaway and thinks of "Crossbuns" ("small cakes especially prepared for Good Friday and appropriately marked with a cross" [*NJ* 127]); his first gesture after buying the cakes is to break "the brittle paste" (*U* 124–25). In "Wandering Rocks," Boody (her name a pun on both "body" and "blood") breaks "big chunks of bread into the yellow soup," while re-

citing "Our Father who are not in heaven" (*U* 186). Since
communion in the Catholic Mass is considered to begin with
the Lord's Prayer (a preparation for the ceremony), with this
allusion Boody invites us to regard her repast as a secular
eucharist; then her sarcasm defeats the point.

If in *A Portrait* Joyce modulates between the Eucharist as
Real Presence of Christ and as powerful symbol, in *Ulysses*
he modulates between the Eucharist as powerful symbol and
no symbol at all. The question is perhaps whether remysti-
fication takes place. But it seems to me that instead religious
significance dwindles, that the spreading out of Eucharistic
signs results in an attenuation of the sacrament's force. Just
as Joyce's bread-eating characters range from major to minor
figures, the bread that may be seen as analogous to the host
itself ranges quantitatively from whole slices to mere crumbs.
Master Patrick Aloysius Dignam finds himself bored by Mrs.
Stoer, Mrs. Quigley, and Mrs. MacDowell, who sip sherry
and eat "crumbs of the cottage fruitcake" (*U* 206). Martin
Cunningham brushes off what are said (perhaps euphemistically) to be "crustcrumbs" from the carriage seat in "Hades"
(*U* 74). And apparently so much bread is eaten in Molly and
Bloom's bed that the "woollen mattress" in "Ithaca" is dubbed
the "biscuit section" (*U* 599); Bloom's legs, when extended
on it, encounter, predictably, "some crumbs" (*U* 601). One
could argue that, slight as these eucharistic signs may seem,
they serve Joyce's aim to spread the Mystery of the Eucharist
to even the most trivial things better than would more dignified
bread imagery. Yet one would not want naively to miss the
joke, as many as these "crustcrumbs" and "crumbs" are apt
to be semen rather than eucharistic bread. (Here the host truly,
as Stephen says in *A Portrait*, "crumble[s] into corruption"
[*P* 106].) As always, Joyce replaces theology with sexuality.

Still, bread imagery in *Ulysses* can seem irrepressible; Joyce
has made a fetish of it. Besides being eaten, bread is delivered,
smelled, sung about, fed to birds, and sold in the novel, in

contexts moreover that strive to recuperate it for theology. In "Hades," a hawker sells "Simnel cakes . . . cakes for the dead" that are in addition termed "Dogbiscuits" (*U* 83)—anagram in *Ulysses* for "Godbiscuits." Herein lie further spreading and the concomitant dwindling: located earlier in semen, the Eucharist now reduces to dogbiscuits, if one accepts the anagrammatic troping. Joyce makes disregarding the Eucharistic allusion of bread imagery an untenable position, even as he refuses to give us sufficient evidence that we are seeing anything more than the *accidents* of the Eucharist, its empty shell, its (dog's) body and not its (God's) Body, the *letter* of divinity (d-o-g = g-o-d) but not the spirit.

Blood works the same duplicitous way. Bread imagery is complemented in *Ulysses* naturally by blood imagery, a pairing that itself suggests the Eucharist in secular form. Musing on the idea that "Chinese cemeteries with giant poppies growing produce the best opium" and noting the proximity of the Botanic Gardens to the cemetery in "Hades," Bloom decides, "It's the blood sinking in the earth gives new life." If we are slow or reluctant to find in Bloom's speculation an analogy to the spiritually renewing blood of Jesus, Bloom supplies the necessary connective: "Same idea those jews they said killed the christian boy" (*U* 89). In reasoning to himself about the fallacious conclusions that George Lidwell and Lydia Douce arrive at as they hold the shell up to their ears in "Sirens," Bloom fixes on the subject of blood: "The sea they think they hear. Singing. A roar. The blood it is. Souse in the ear sometimes. Well, it's a sea. Corpuscle islands" (*U* 231). His last image expands his meaning, catapulting us back to the first scene of the book in which Buck struggles to transubstantiate shaving lather to "white corpuscles" (*U* 3). At Barney Kiernan's, again preoccupied with "the circulation of the blood," Bloom tries to force the subject into the general conversation; although he is not given a chance to develop a parallel between human blood and the blood of Christ, the ensuing references to Dublin's "pet lamb" and "the lamb" (the nicknames of a prizefighter) (*U* 261, 262) nevertheless make the analogy by subliminal association.

Gradually the theological significance of Eucharistic images in *Ulysses* flickers and fades away into the writing, into the Text. To persist in locating the sacrament in Joyce's teasing secular eucharistic imagery and puns is to be as deluded as George and Lydia hearing the sea in her empty shell. Joyce carries such references to their limit. In "Lestrygonians," Paddy Leonard vents his annoyance with Bloom for Bloom's supposed secret knowledge of the Gold cup race in language with latent religious connotations: "He has some bloody horse up his sleeve for the Gold cup" (*U* 146). Especially because of the combination of references—to blood as well as a gold cup—we may find in Leonard's statement the faintest allusion to the blood of Christ contained in the chalice. It seems there and not there. The word "bloody"—Joyce certainly knew the false etymology of God's blood—is overindulged by the "Cyclops" narrator and characters alike. In a short paragraph describing Bob Doran's shenanigans with Garryowen as well as the dog's ravenous eating, the word crops up five times. At one point it is used specifically to describe the "dog," anagram of "God"; and its repetitions cluster around another ubiquitous eucharistic word, biscuit:

Arrah, bloody end to the paw he'd paw and Alf trying to keep him from tumbling off the bloody stool atop of the bloody old dog and he talking all kinds of drivel about training by kindness and thoroughbred dog and intelligent dog: give you the bloody pip. Then he starts scraping a few bits of old biscuit out of the bottom of a Jacobs' tin he told Terry to bring. Gob, he golloped it down like old boots and his tongue hanging out of him a yard long for more. Near ate the tin and all, hungry bloody mongrel. [*U* 251]

The citizen highlights the half-alive religious puns in this passage by threatening to "By Jesus . . . brain that bloody jewman," to "By Jesus . . . crucify him," and by asking for the "biscuitbox" to facilitate his effort (*U* 280). This same biscuit tin is soon thereafter described as "the bloody tin" (*U* 281); hence bread and blood images vacuously converge.

Joyce's "theological" puns end up inciting us to read against the theology, as well as against the narrative, of the fathers/ Fathers, as the Mystery of the Eucharist is subsumed within the acrobatics of Joyce's writing. At the end of "Oxen," someone cries out "Landlord, landlord, have you good wine, staboo?" (*U* 348); and a pun that follows, "Cot's plood" ("dialect for the oath 'God's blood' " [*NJ* 367]), also invokes the blood of the Lord. "Circe" begins as "*stunted men and women . . . grab wafers between which are wedged lumps of coral and copper snow*" (*U* 350). And Joyce puns on "host" repeatedly in "Ithaca." The repetition alone has the effect of stressing while hollowing out the word. Only the linguistic clothing, and not the embodiment, of the Eucharist remains.

Underlining the point of empty homological compatibility (between the Eucharist and Joyce's language), there is yet another odd twist of Joyce's secularizing, demystifying screw. That Throwaway has won the Gold cup prompts Lenehan to remark, "Takes the biscuit" (*U* 267). The cliché is literalized by the actual biscuit tin that receives so much attention in "Cyclops": immediately after blurting out the cliché (as if to guarantee that we notice its literalization), Lenehan walks "over to the biscuit tin" (*U* 267). Likewise, in "Eumaeus," Bloom jokes to Stephen that Mulligan "knows which side his bread is buttered on" (*U* 507); and in "Telemachus" (as Kenner once amusedly observed), Mulligan had "filled his mouth with a crust thickly buttered on both sides" (*U* 13). Just as I have been drawing possible references to the Eucharist from language ostensibly unrelated to this ritual, Joyce appears to be signaling that there are secular hosts in these clichés about bread (this "accident" is not accidental here). For in each case he juxtaposes a purely linguistic reality—the clichés themselves—with something real—a biscuit and bread—so that, as in the Eucharist, something intangible resides side by side with something tangible. That is to say, Christ sacramentally in the host corresponds with the ideational content conveyed by the clichés "Takes the biscuit" and "He knows which side his bread is buttered on"; and the accidents of the bread correspond with the biscuit and bread apparent in, but not substantially informing, the clichés. As part of Lenehan's and Bloom's clichés, the biscuit and bread are accidental—the efficacy of these clichés is not dependent on a real biscuit or bread. Yet, while this parallel does suggest itself, it hints of a strain. It barely holds up, although it seems to me valid enough to enable Joyce to "lower" the Eucharist to the level of jokes on clichés. Still, we may wish to ask: Are we in the presence of a lapsed Catholic who at every moment is shedding or failing to shed his Catholicism? The undecidability of this intractable question—or undecidability per se—is perhaps the secret of Joyce's rebellion.

Having shifted from theology to wordplay and in turn to undecidability, we might expect to encounter the woman. "That which will not be pinned down by truth is, in truth— *feminine*," pronounces Derrida,[6] and of course even some, especially French, feminists champion this conception. Molly's blood has notoriously been compared with Christ's. There is even more evidence to support the analogy than what Ellmann has gathered.[7] Pondering in "Lestrygonians" the rapidity with which babies are born into the world, Bloom marvels, "One born every second somewhere. Other dying every second. Since I fed the birds five minutes. Three hundred kicked the bucket. Other three hundred born." Then for no apparent reason, except perhaps that the sentiments and language of Dowie's throwaway are fresh on his mind, Bloom finishes off his thoughts with: "Washing the blood off, all are washed in the blood of the lamb, bawling maaaaaa" (*U* 134–35). The blood of woman and the blood of the lamb coalesce.

Christ's blood blends with Molly's/woman's blood, and flowers thereby acquire a religious connotation. In referring euphemistically to Martha's menstrual cycle with the line "Has her roses probably" (*U* 64), Bloom conflates woman's blood and flowers. (The word "flower" is used to refer to menstruation in the Bible,[8] and the O.E.D. gives "menses" as an obsolete meaning.) Roses and blood are juxtaposed in the *"womancity"* in "Circe": *"Mammoth roses murmur of scarlet winegrapes. A wine of shame, lust, blood exudes, strangely murmuring"* (*U* 389). Flowers preside as wine becomes blood; they murmur as if joined in the celebration of some profanely eucharistic rite.

Once we recognize woman's blood and flowers as secular eucharistic signs, *Ulysses* (almost every chapter an organ, none of which is solely male, including even "Lotus-Eaters," which is assigned the bisexual or vague "genitals") may appear as an enormous spiritualized female body. All three of the main female characters—Martha, Gerty, and Molly—menstruate during the book. And flowers are virtually ubiquitous. They are established as synecdoches of women: in "Douce Lydia. Bronze and rose" (*U* 230), "rose" is a sort of badge of Lydia Douce's identity; and Molly states outright of herself, "I was a Flower of the mountain yes when I put the rose in my hair," and of women in general, "we are flowers all" (*U* 643). This metonymy ramifies. If flowers/women hold sacramental value, Henry Flower, the Rose of Castile, Boylan's carnation, in sum, the entire linguistic floral world of *Ulysses* gains sacramental significance. Even more religious illumination can be shed on Boylan's flower. The word "carnation" derives from the Latin word for flesh, *"carnis,"* and therefore by implication incarnates not only blood but body. The eucharistic linguistic power of woman in this novel is so extensive that it can bestow holiness on Blazes Boylan.

And so again we find ourselves locating religious sentiment in the play of language, play set in motion by a slide from Christ's to Molly's blood. But play—like the menstrual blood of women, or women themselves (if one accepts Nietzsche's view), and perhaps even the frail flower—was alien to the stern Fathers of Dublin who stood for Catholicism in Joyce's eyes, and who employed the pandybat to punish disobedience of their law. By stretching the sacrament of the Eucharist to menstrual blood, flowers, and puns (all in one swoop), by placing references to the Mystery in contexts so removed from it (even threatening to it) that its force is severely attenuated, if not lost, Joyce challenges insidiously the Fathers' law.

II

[Stephen] begs his mother to tell him the word that is
"known to all men" . . . and that demand is for a word
that will come complete with its own meaning, eliminat-
ing the hazardous world of the signifier where he is at
the mercy of chance. But the name he must come to
learn is a signifier in excess of a signified, a name in ex-
cess of its bearer: the Name of the Father.
—MacCabe, *James Joyce and the Revolution of the*
    Word

My argument that the Eucharist suffers dissolution within the play of Joyce's language should not be taken to imply that Joyce approached this Mystery in a dilettantish manner. We know that he was familiar with the rigorous questions concerning the Eucharist that Aquinas poses, since in chapter III of *A Portrait*, Stephen's mind winds "itself in and out of the curious [theological] questions proposed to it," many of which have to do with the Eucharist and are generated by Aquinas's discussion in the *Summa Theologica*. Stephen queries:

> Why was the sacrament of the eucharist instituted under
> the two species of bread and wine if Jesus Christ be present
> body and blood, soul and divinity, in the bread alone and
> in the wine alone? Does a tiny particle of the consecrated
> bread contain all the body and blood of Jesus Christ or a
> part only of the body and blood? If the wine change into
> vinegar and the host crumble into corruption after they have
> been consecrated is Jesus Christ still present under their
> species as God and as man? [P 106][9]

Several scenes of *Ulysses* testify that Joyce had more than a
rudimentary knowledge of the history of theological controversies surrounding the Eucharist. It seems, in fact, that in an
effort to establish the correct (Church) version of the model
on which he bases his art (the Eucharist too has a realistic/
suprarealistic organization), Joyce presents in *Ulysses* erroneous conceptions of this Mystery by way of contrast. He
goes to great lengths to get the precise analogy before ex-
ploding it. As always, Joyce—an apostate, not a heretic—finds
the forms his rebellion might take in the very object of his
rebellion.

In *The Eucharist,* Edward Schillebeeckx describes a heretical
theory of the Eucharist called " 'sensualistic' interpretation,"
which prevailed during the Middle Ages just prior to Aquinas
and which Aquinas felt the need to abrogate. The sensualists
took the idea of the presence of Christ in the Eucharist too
corporeally, as if it meant that one could make physical contact
with Him. They thought, for example, that the recipient of
the host actually bites the body of Christ, and that "whenever
unbelievers pricked consecrated hosts, in hatred or a desire
to inflict torture, and the hosts began, according to the medieval legends, to bleed, this 'blood' was really the true blood
of Christ." But St. Thomas, as Schillebeeckx puts it, "was
unable to accept this gross realism." Aquinas asserted that
"we do not crush Christ with our teeth—'Christ is not eaten

and chewed with the teeth in his corporeality, but in sacramental forms.' " To priests "who drank the consecrated wine and then apparently became tortured by uncertainty because they tasted wine and not blood," Aquinas explained that "what they tasted was no deceit—what they drank was 'a *sacramentum* of Christ's blood.' "[10]

Aquinas writes that in the Eucharist "the whole substance of the bread is changed into the whole substance of Christ's body, and the whole substance of the wine into the whole substance of Christ's blood." It is a substantial change that takes place: hence the term *"transubstantiation"* (*ST*, III, Q. 75, Art. 4). What the sensualists and Bloom (in his notion of Eucharistic cannibalism) fail to understand, and what Buck Mulligan appears willfully to misunderstand, is that the "accidents of the bread and wine remain after the consecration" (*ST*, III, Q. 75, Art. 5)—one can make physical contact with them alone. It is true that the accidents of Christ's body are also in the Eucharist, but only

> by means of the substance; so that the accidents of Christ's body have no immediate relationship either to this sacrament or to adjacent bodies; consequently they do not act on the medium so as to be seen by any corporeal eye. . . . Christ's body is substantially present in this sacrament. But substance, as such, is not visible to the bodily eye, nor does it come under any one of the senses, nor under the imagination, but solely under the intellect, whose object is *what a thing is* (*De Anima*. iii). [*ST*, III, Q. 76, Art. 7]

It would consequently be impossible to bite into Christ and torture him.

In the opening scene of *Ulysses,* Buck Mulligan falsifies the Eucharist by assuming that through his conversion Christ's "body and soul and blood and ouns" will enter his shaving bowl–chalice. That Buck has "a little trouble about those white corpuscles" (*U* 3) makes vivid the point that he is at-

tempting to get in bit by bit all of Christ's accidents quantitatively rather than substantially ("by means of the substance,"
of which one can have only intellectual knowledge). Buck acts
out a sensualist communion in order ultimately to scoff at the
idea of the Real Presence. His most obvious pose is as a scientific priest who attempts to effect transubstantiation by
means of electricity, the final words of his service being
"Switch off the current, will you?" (*U* 3). But, as all Catholic
theologians would doubtless assert, "Transsubstantiation . . .
is a religious reality, not a natural phenomenon"; "There is
no physical change; there is no chemical change. One can never
discern the presence of Christ physically or chemically, not
even with the electronic microscope."[11]

In Buck's hands, the sensualist heresy reduces to a predis-
position to dwell on matter at the expense of spirit. If we
translate his "sin of materialism" into literary terms, it becomes apparent that Joyce himself may have verged on com-
mitting a related heresy by virtue of his outpouring of naturalistic writing—the literary style I have identified as part of
his legacy from the fathers/Fathers. (Though in another context sensualism would probably not be aligned with naturalism—we would never think to say, for instance, that Zola
commits a literary sensualist heresy—this correspondence may
be made with respect to *Ulysses,* since by giving the sensualist
perspective to some of his characters, in a work that is at least
initially heavily naturalistic, Joyce himself suggests the parallel.
It seems plausible since both sensualism and naturalism stress
accidents—sensualists by emphasizing Christ's corporeal
presence in the consecrated bread and wine, naturalists by
having no conception of another world, substantial or spiritual, beyond the accidents.) But Joyce eventually links Buck
to the sadistic Dublin priests conducting a black mass in
"Circe," thereby confirming that naturalism is a literary form
of sensualism and simultaneously distancing himself from it.
He thus reinforces MacCabe's proposition that representa-

tional writing maintains the power of the (in this case, perverted) priest.

The "Circean" mass extends unmistakably Mulligan's service. The initials of Buck Mulligan's name echo the beginning letters of the words "black mass"; Father Malachi O'Flynn's first name also brings Buck into the "Circe" mass, perhaps revealing him to be the "Circean" celebrant.[12] With the demonic mass of "Circe," the ribaldry of Buck's service turns to obscenity. Where Buck chants *"Introibo ad altare Dei"* (with an implicit blasphemy), Father O'Flynn chants *"Introibo ad altare diaboli"* (in his explicit diabolism). Buck in "Telemachus" wears (merely) an "ungirdled" dressinggown; *"On the altarstone* [in "Circe"] *Mrs Mina Purefoy, goddess of unreason, lies, naked, fettered, a chalice resting on her swollen belly,"* and the Reverend Mr. Haines Love *"raises high behind the celebrant's petticoat, revealing his grey bare hairy buttocks behind which a carrot is stuck."* While Buck fools innocuously with shaving foam (*U* 3), Father O'Flynn *"elevates a blooddripping host"* (*U* 489). Herein lies a vital intensification. Father O'Flynn's mass is so crude that sensualism stands revealed as sadism. The lineage commencing with the pederast in "An Encounter" and including all the punishing patriarchs of *Dubliners* as well as the flogging Fathers of *A Portrait* reaches a climax. This antireligious rite, the black mass of "Circe," despite its ostensible antithetical position vis-à-vis the Church, turns out to reproduce the perverse atmosphere of Catholic Dublin that Stephen and Joyce experienced. With his *"grey bare hairy buttocks"* on show, the celebrant even seems poised to be pandied.

Buck's blasphemy has no appeal for Joyce. It is shown to be akin to a sick ritual that extends the sadistic world of whipping in *Dubliners* and *A Portrait*. And, as it takes the form of sensualism whose rhetorical alter ego, as we have seen, is naturalism with its insistence on one-to-one subordination of words to things, the phallic Buck is further condemned. In-

dicting Buck, MacCabe writes, "Buck Mulligan, as his nick-
name implies, stands for a phallic world that can ignore the
possibility of difference because it is confident of its unchal-
lengeable possession of the phallus" (MacCabe 107). Joyce
repudiates all of this—materialism/naturalism, the phallic and
the sadistic—in his pursuit of more subtle delights, linguistic
delights that become available to him through the grueling
process of excavating the Eucharistic/eucharistic images he first
produces.

Having wrestled with and having disavowed naturalism in
"Circe," *Ulysses* is free to feature secular eucharists modeled
on the proper—not a sensualist—version of the Church Mystery. Joyce's privileged secular eucharists, then, would entail
something more than realism. To see how they do, we need
to notice that the language Joyce uses to construct the famous
communions in "Eumaeus" and "Ithaca" has as its paradigm
the accidents-substance structure of the Eucharist; the scenes
themselves give rise to this asseveration.

In the "Eumaeus" communion scene, Bloom pushes surrep-
titiously "the cup of what was temporarily supposed to be
called coffee gradually nearer [Stephen]." After Stephen's short
speech on the deceptive nature of sounds as well as names,
and an expression of concurrence from Bloom, not only the
true identity of the coffee but of the roll as well is in question:
Bloom also pushes "the socalled roll across" (*U* 509). On the
literal level, "coffee" and "roll" are dubious labels for the
drink and food placed before Bloom and Stephen probably
because of the poor quality of the fare at the cabman's shelter;
the sarcastically described "boiling swimming cup of a choice
concoction labelled coffee" and "rather antediluvian specimen
of a bun" (*U* 622) hardly resemble what coffee and a bun (or
roll) ideally look like. On another level, though, these expres-
sions of doubt may indicate that the coffee and roll are not
what they seem, are masking their true reality, and are therefore only accidentally coffee and bread, supplying the external

body of an invisible presence. Invoking religion directly, one of the names Stephen lists as an "imposture" is "Jesus" (*U* 509)—an impostor, posing variously as a man, and as bread and wine, whose duplicity has the best theological justifications. A second fairly blatant clue that we are to think of the difference between the nominal coffee and roll and another reality they possess as having a Eucharistic homologue is the last word of the phrase "the socalled roll across." As Joyce surely knew from the *Summa* (if from no other source), Christ crucified is contained in the sacrament of the Eucharist (*ST*, III, Q. 73, Art. 6).

Not only then do the words of this scene derive from, refer to, and embody aspects of the Eucharist—as we have learned from Tindall, "coffee" "comes from the Arabic word for wine";[13] "the socalled roll" may suggest another secular host; and "across" houses the word "cross"—but the relationship of the apparent meaning of each of these words or phrases to its more recondite, religious meaning is homologous with the structure of the Eucharist. The actual coffee and roll are to their "spiritual" meanings of "wine" (the reader who locates wine in "coffee" performs an act analogous to that of the communicant who accepts wine for blood) and "host," as the accidents of bread and wine are to the substantial presence of Christ in the Eucharist. The word "across," understood in terms of its literal meaning, may be regarded similarly as an accidental denotation masking a substantial and spiritual connotation, the cross of the crucifixion.

This division of language into accidents and substance persists in the "Ithaca" communion scene. Like "the cup of what was temporarily supposed to be called coffee" and "the socalled roll" of "Eumaeus," here "host," "massproduct," and "cocoa," understood representationally, serve as accidents for their respective spiritual meanings of eucharistic wafer, the product of the Mass, and "god food" ("cocoa is *'theobroma'* to botanists; and *'theobroma'* is Greek for 'god food' ").[14]

Joyce reinforces our sense of the insubstantial (and therefore accidental) ontology of the cocoa by bringing the "label" of Epps's cocoa into sharp focus: Bloom proceeds "according to the directions for use printed on the label" (*U* 553). Likewise, in the "Eumaeus" scene, the point is made implicitly that the coffee served at the shelter is merely "labelled" coffee (*U* 509), hinting at a possible gap between what is written on the container and what is contained.

But the gap between Joyce's secular eucharistic accidents (say, the word "across") and substance (in this case the cross of the crucifixion) becomes so gaping, so abysmal that, despite the apparent affinity between the way Joyce's language is constructed and the structure of the Eucharist, religious meaning drops out of the picture. Joyce uses the Eucharist as a linguistic model even as he pries open the accidents-substance relationship to the point that it splits. That the cross of the crucifixion is lodged within the word "across" has perhaps a short-lived or ghostly theological significance; but what is most notable is that through this "trick" of Joyce's language, Christ's crucifixion gets absorbed into a word game. The pun in the end undermines the privileged status of Christ's death on the cross, as it yokes it together with the more common meaning of the word "across"; the religious connotation of "cross" becomes just one of the paronomastic referents. Likewise, one (and only one) meaning of "host," "massproduct," and "cocoa" is theological; the theological referent is forced linguistically to take its humble place among other possible referents, and in some cases among several of them. It joins a relay of signifiers rather than reigns supreme over them. If we regard Catholic theology in general as constitutive symbolically of the Father, we can see that this is exactly what MacCabe, to hark back to the epigraph of this section, thinks Stephen needed to learn: "a signifier in excess of a signified, a name in excess of its bearer: the Name of the Father" (MacCabe 129). It is God's very name "God" that early in *A Portrait* Stephen clings to ("still God remained always the same God and God's real name was God") even though on the verge of discerning the possibility of a linguistic splintering of the Father: "God was God's name just as his name was Stephen. *Dieu* was the French for God and that was God's name too. . . . [T]here were different names for God in all the different languages in the world" (*P* 16). Acting on Stephen's repressed insight that "God" is a linguistic tag rather than an essence, Joyce uses puns to relegate the Father to his legal (fictional) status as name, one among many.

That such excess, a relay of signifiers rather than a hierarchical linguistic structure, was associated in Joyce's mind with the feminine can once again be demonstrated by a turn to Molly Bloom. For she confects the last nonliteral eucharist of the novel, in a gesture that consecrates Bloom's proposal of marriage: "The day I got him to propose to me yes first I gave him the bit of seedcake out of my mouth . . ." (*U* 643). Molly substitutes herself for the priest, placing sensuously the "host" in Bloom's mouth, from her own mouth, as if to offer a "bit" from her own body. It is her voluptuous body (and not Christ's) that looms into focus to comprise the ultimate scene of the book. As if to link the "seedcake" to her body, Molly thinks (directly after her memory of transferring the seedcake to Bloom): "Yes he said I was a flower of the mountain yes so we are flowers all a womans body yes that was one true thing he said in his life" (*U* 643). "Seedcake," then, is eucharistic if we read it figuratively; and the body that produces it belongs to the novel's mistress of the language of play. Molly replaces Christ, as the figural supplants the literal. The last few notes of the book are a paean to her body and, insofar as she is a flower and is menstruating, her blood.

III

[Joyce] said to Frank Budgen, "The Holy Roman Catholic Apostolic Church was built on a pun. It ought to be good enough for me." To the objection of triviality, he

> replied, "Yes. Some of the means I use are trivial—and
> some are quadrivial."
> —Ellmann, *James Joyce*

Joyce gets to women via the Incarnation with even more speed
than he does via the Eucharist. He juxtaposes his versions of
the two Mysteries in Stephen's Last Supper service in "Oxen."
Stephen's eucharistic consecration—"Now drink we, quod he,
of this mazer and quaff ye this mead which is not indeed parcel
of my body but my soul's bodiment"—is followed by words
whose relationship to the Gospel According to St. John is obvious—"In woman's womb word is made flesh but in the spirit
of the maker all flesh that passes becomes the word that shall
not pass away. This is the postcreation" (*U* 320). Joyce takes
the idea of the Incarnation, reverses it, and uses the reversal
as a metaphor to suggest his artistic transformation of real
life to the "womb of the imagination," where it is transfigured
and immortalized. He seems to be especially attracted to the
theological notion that it is part of the essence of the Incarnation that the Word that becomes flesh never ceases to be
the Word, since his reversal of the Incarnation reveals his desire
to travel in the direction of a womb-like linguistic space. Joyce
even dramatizes in *Ulysses* his secularized version of the In-
carnation-in-reverse by moving, through Stephen and Bloom,
away from his mother and her real womb ("In woman's womb
word is made flesh") to a surrendering of himself to the
"womb of the imagination" ("but in the spirit of the maker
all flesh that passes becomes the word that shall not pass
away") as it is embodied in "Penelope." From flesh to word,
Logos to logos, phallus to "womb of the imagination."

Stephen is famously preoccupied with his mother in the Telemachiad: she haunts him, as we know, in one very lucid
dream ("her wasted body within its loose brown graveclothes
giving off an odour of wax and rosewood, her breath, that
had bent upon him, mute, reproachful, a faint odour of wetted

ashes" [*U* 5]). In his daydreams she cries, "For those words,
Stephen: love's bitter mystery" (*U* 8). Stephen's speculation
that the only real and true thing in life is *"Amor matris"* (*U*
23) shows his troubled devotion. And he is plagued by memories of the telegram his father sent him in Paris that told of
his mother's dying state, as well as by recollections of Mulligan's aunt's charge—"You killed your mother" (*U* 35).
Joyce's complicity in Stephen's struggle with the real mother
is implied by the immanence of May Dedalus's spirit in the
fictional landscape of the Telemachiad. Stephen is not long at
breakfast when an avatar of his mother appears: the aged
milkwoman with, as Stephen notices, "old shrunken paps,"
who is said to enter "from a morning [a possible pun on
"mourning"] world" as "maybe a messenger" (*U* 12). And
Stephen's receptivity to the sea, "our mighty mother"—at the
end of "Telemachus," a voice calls from the water, and he
waves—might be read as a manifestation of his wish to crawl
back into his mother's womb.

But Stephen's vampire-like fantasy, at the end of "Proteus,"
casts into doubt the possibility of that desire: "His lips lipped
and mouthed fleshless lips of air: mouth to her moomb. Oomb,
allwombing tomb" (*U* 40). Stephen imagines preying gro-
tesquely upon the real mother's womb, a locus of horror and
death. In "Circe," when the apparition of May Dedalus looms
up and reminds Stephen of her love—she tells him, as if en-
ticingly, "Years and years I loved you, O, my son, my firstborn,
when you lay in my womb" (*U* 474)—Stephen (and Joyce
through Stephen) steels himself against her. He shouts out the
rebellious, Satanic words *"Non serviam!"* (*U* 475), smashing
the chandelier with his ashplant (possibly in an attempt to
kill the ghost). Anti-Oedipal Stephen has no qualms about
employing his ashplant—corollary of the fathers'/Fathers'
whip/pandybat—to fend off the real mother whom he resented
in her role as agent of the punishing (religious) patriarchy. To
Stephen she is a "corpsechewer!"—"*A green crab with ma-*

lignant red eyes [that] *sticks deep its grinning claws in Stephen's heart*" (*U* 474–75).

Joyce's rejection of the real womb via Stephen releases him to pursue the imaginary womb, the womb of writing, to which he proceeds through Bloom, "the childman weary, the manchild in the womb," traveling to a "dark bed" (*U* 606–07). For Joyce's coda is metaphorized aptly as a womb of words, a dense, dark, sensuous, and sensual cavern composed of words "that shall not pass away," composed too of the novel's most joyful language. And so once again we arrive at language of play ("Penelope"—about which I will speak extensively later on), as does Joyce over and over, through the refashioning of a Church Mystery.

Yet it has not been left exclusively to Joyce to generate wordplay from the Incarnation. Even this Joycean lever against the Fathers may be traced back to the Church, despite the apparent tendency in both the Church Fathers and the classic writers of the Middle Ages to equate "women with the illusory" so that "the discourse of misogyny then becomes a plaint against . . . writing itself," as R. Howard Bloch argues.[15] Father Ong (in "Wit and Mystery: A Revaluation in Mediaeval Latin Hymnody") shows that puns on the Incarnation are prevalent in Aquinas's poetry. A well-known instance may be found in a couplet in the Vesper hymn *Pange Lingua*, written for the office of Corpus Christi: "Verbum caro panem verum / Verbo carnem efficit." "Thomas is here concerned with the fact that it was not God the Father nor God the Holy Spirit, but the Second Person, God the Word, Who became flesh, and that this same Word, when He wishes to convert bread into His flesh uses *words* as the instruments for His action."[16] The theology of the Incarnation has provided conceits for medieval theologians as well as patristic rhetoricians, seventeenth-century Englishmen, and contemporary poets who identify with the metaphysical tradition. Ong traces (for example) the conceit/paradox of the "*Verbum infans,* Who was not only the infant Word, the child Jesus, but, to take the Latin _infans_ in its full etymological force, the unspeaking Word," through St. Augustine, Aquinas, Lancelot Andrewes, and T. S. Eliot.[17]

But Joyce not only puns on the Incarnation—most notably in Stephen's postcreation speech (also on "word"). He had to exceed mere paronomastic pleasure, knowing the Church was founded on a pun. For one thing, he makes an original contribution to this history of the relationship of the pun and the Incarnation—one that enables him again to stretch the connection between a Church Mystery and linguistic play to the vanishing point. _Ulysses_ treats the pun itself as a logological equivalent (to borrow a concept from Kenneth Burke) to the Incarnation.

We know that Joyce's secularization of the Eucharist eventually spills into puns. And although a parallel between the pun and the Eucharist may be said to exist since the Eucharist, like the pun, contains dissimilarities—in the case of the Eucharist, accidents and substance; in the case of the pun, two or more unrelated meanings—the more exact affinity is with the Incarnation. (The pun's homological relationship to the Eucharist, I would argue, shows by contrast the fineness of its connection with the Incarnation.) If we press the analogy, we see that the pun does not function in a way strictly congruent with the relationship of Eucharistic accidents and substance. All the meanings of a pun, one would have to say, are "substantially" rather than "accidentally" present in the sense that in constituting the identity of the pun (qua pun) no one meaning takes hierarchical precedence over any other (even though all meanings of course dwell in the frame of one word which may register a single apparent, representational meaning), and since it is a question of the annexing of one linguistic reality with another, whereas in the Eucharist the substance of Christ is certainly privileged over the accidents of bread and wine. That is, the pun joins referents solely on the linguistic level; the only way the words that comprise a pun can coalesce is as words. The pun does not fuse linguistic and real—as it were substantial and accidental—levels in any special way. The pun's structure, however, corresponds rather neatly with that of the Incarnation, since Christ is substantially God and substantially man, though for practical purposes he inhabited the frame of a man.

Beyond this, the Eucharist involves a transubstantiation process to which there is no equivalent in the pun, since no one meaning yields to any other. But in the Incarnation, "the Divine Nature is said to be incarnate because It is united to flesh personally, and not that It is changed into flesh. So likewise the flesh is said to be deified . . . not by change, but by union with the Word, its natural properties still remaining" (*ST*, III, Q. 2, Art. 1). As in the pun, in which two or more meanings reside in one word-frame, in the Incarnation *"two natures"* (each of which retains its identity) are united in *"one hypostasis"* or person (*ST*, III, Q. 2, Art. 3).

Perhaps these homological affinities between the Incarnation and the pun even account for the widespread punning of writers preoccupied with the Incarnation: it seems possible that the incongruous religious conjoining fostered the incongruous literary conjoining. The pun makes a dazzling appearance, for instance, in Donne and Hopkins, both of whom were far from being Arians or Unitarians. Perhaps, similarly, this structural compatibility explains the rash of puns that occurs just prior to Stephen's postcreation speech. Two puns stand out on Bloom's name alone. It is asked "of sir Leopold would he in like case so jeopard" the life of a mother to save the life of her child: here "jeopard" is used to mean "jeopardize," and, as "jeopard" resembles "leopard," to play on Bloom's name "Leopold." Not only does "leopard" look like "Leopold," but Bloom, as the plot of *Ulysses* reveals, is the "black panther" or "leopard" that Haines dreams about. And Dixon at one point comments, "That is truth, pardy" (*U* 319), possibly intending with the word "pardy" to ejaculate "a mild oath" (the meaning Webster's dictionary gives for "pardie," that is, "par Dieu"), or, as the word "pardy" which contains "pard" may be expanded to "leopard" ("pard" is an archaism for "leopard"), to joke again on Bloom's name. Joyce hints at the link between these vulgar puns and the Church by including in the same passage the founding Catholic pun, the pun on *Peter's* name: Stephen looks to "that blessed Peter on which rock was holy church for all ages founded" for confirmation of his views on birth control and related matters (*U* 319).

Joyce tightens the relationship between the pun and the Incarnation with puns on birth (also made just prior to the postcreation speech). "Delivirly" is used in a phrase describing Bloom—"and in such sort delivirly he scaped their questions"—as an archaism for "deftly," and to allude to the act of giving birth. And Dixon remarks, "That is truth, pardy . . . or I err, a pregnant word" (*U* 319). These allusions to pregnancy and birth certainly have a local relevance in this chapter, since at the time they are made, Mrs. Purefoy is within less than an hour of her delivery. But there is also good reason for regarding them as allusions to the Virgin birth. Dixon's pun—"a pregnant word"—suggests implicitly the pregnancy that incarnated the Word. And a conceptual pun runs throughout this section on mothers—uniting Eve (referred to as "the thorntree" as against "the rose upon the rood of time"), the rose herself (Mary), the "Mother Church," and "Marion"—which tends to turn all maternity into prefigurations or postfigurations of Mary's maternity. Mrs. Purefoy, given her name, must be taken as a type of, or pun on, the Virgin.

It is rebellious enough that Joyce plays as extravagantly as he does on the paronomastic possibilities of the Incarnation. Although for centuries it had been considered perfectly pious to pun on the Incarnation, most of Joyce's puns surrounding and seemingly sparked by Stephen's Incarnation speech are derisive of Catholic theology. What provides a basis of comparison in the first place in the end produces only alienation. But an even more effective and radical strategy for distancing himself from his various Fathers lies again in Joyce's turn to women, a turn his Incarnational wordplay enables him to take. By means of his extension of medieval punning on the Incarnation, Joyce appropriates the pun from the Fathers; he then uses the pun as a logological equivalent to the Incarnation, which equivalence results in an explosion of puns, including a series of Incarnational puns on birth that reaffirms the kinship in Joyce's writing between women and linguistic play, a kinship crystallized in Joyce's metaphoric designation and destination, the "womb of the imagination." Punning then on women themselves (the mark of the relation between women and wordplay is not simply a matter of metonymic linkage), Joyce reaffirms his conflation of women and signification beyond representation, of women and linguistic extravagance.

Joyce seems not only alert to the subversive strength of "woman" in language but to the sensitivity of Patristic and Medieval theologians to this strength. Using Eve to explain the threat, R. Howard Bloch writes in "Medieval Misogyny" that the relation of Adam to Eve is of "the proper to the figural, which implies always derivation, deflection, denaturing, a tropological turning away. The perversity of Eve is that of the lateral: as the outgrowth of Adam's flank, his *latus,* she retains the status of *translatio,* of translation, transfer, metaphor, trope. She is a side-issue." It is as if Joyce teases out the woman within the supplemental aspect of language as part of his plan to unhinge the very theologians who sensed (and in their own writing flirted with, as Bloch acknowledges) such a threat in the first place. "Verbal signs, in particular," writes Bloch, "stand as a constant reminder of the secondary and supplemental nature of all 'the arts.' 'With the word the garment entered,' Tertullian asserts, implying that language is a covering that, by definition and from the start, is so wrapped up in the decorative as to be essentially perverse." One may or may not wish therefore to conclude, as Bloch does, that literature itself held (holds?) the "danger of woman."[18] But Joyce's turn from Catholicism to language (his textualization of Church Mysteries), though it distances him from Church Fathers, oddly may be a sophisticated form of Mariolatry. I say this not only because Eve, figure of supplementarity, pre-figures the Virgin (and we will see that, in Joyce, Mary's relation to supplementarity is a long story), but also since Joyce's move to language is signaled by a proliferation of images of and puns on the Virgin.

4

The Parturition of the Word: From Logos to logos

I

Thomas Aquinas was the greatest phi-
losopher because his reasoning was
"like a sharp sword." [Joyce] read
him . . . in Latin, a page a day.
—Ellmann, quoting Joyce

"It has been argued," says E. H. Gombrich in *Art and Illusion,* "that the Old Testament ban on 'graven images' is connected not only with a fear of idolatry but with the more universal fear of encroaching on the creator's prerogatives." Certain Jewish households in Poland will admit statuettes only on the condition that "they are not quite complete—if, for instance, a finger is missing." Apparently for the same reason, Jewish manuscripts from the Middle Ages have been found that include figures without faces; it is likely that "the first artist at work in the Synagogue of Duras-Europos of the third century also obeyed similar scruples in his rendering of the sac-

100

rifice of Isaac," for in this wall painting, Isaac's back is turned to us. Gombrich finds evidence of this same fear—of usurping the creator's role—in the Eastern Church: though sacred images eventually were admitted, sculpture in the round—too real to be accepted—was distinguished from painted icons. If the image could be grabbed by the nose, it was anathema.[1]

The Catholic Church, however, fostered no such scruples. What Gombrich reveals about Jewish and Eastern Orthodox attitudes toward art throws a sharp light of contrast on the theology of the Catholic Church, which, far from insisting on God's prerogatives, fueled the desire of artists to emulate Him. In the *Summa,* Aquinas sets up a parallel between the relation of God to His Word, and in turn to His creation, and the relation of the artist to his word, and in turn to his artistic creation: "The craftsman works through the word conceived in his mind, and through the love of his will regarding some object. Hence also God the Father made the creature through His Word, which is His Son; and through His Love, which is the Holy Ghost" (*ST,* I, Q. 45, Art. 6). Aquinas defines for the (Catholic) artist a Godly role to which artists of the Jewish and Eastern Orthodox religions could never aspire.

We know that Joyce studied in the *Summa* at least part of St. Thomas's "Treatise on the Trinity" since the three components of beauty that Stephen delineates in *A Portrait* derive from Aquinas's discussion of the beauty of the Word. Joyce's regard for this Mystery of the Church was not unimpassioned: Leo Manglaviti points out that, according to August Suter's recollection, "Joyce once refused to attend a performance of Bach's *Matthäus-Passion* because the text syncretized the Gospels of Matthew and John." This was upsetting since St. John was for Joyce "the highest attainment of the evangelists"; "he was fond of quoting the opening: 'In the beginning was the Word.' "[2] As for the Third Person: though Joyce hesitated to discuss matters of mere opinion, he was willing to take up seriously the topic of the Procession of the Holy Ghost, since he felt that *"an intellectual background has been created for the doctrine."*[3] Trinitarian theology obviously captured Joyce's attention in artistic and intellectual contexts.

He seems to have cared about it numerically as well. Although in *Ulysses on the Liffey,* Ellmann (via his reference to Dante) only implicitly observes the relevance of the Trinity to Joyce's division of the novel into groups of three (Ellmann finds in each of the three dominant sections of *Ulysses* triads of chapters), it is easy to make the link. Whether or not we agree with Ellmann's dialectical interpretation ("Having adopted the triadic organization, Joyce planned that each triad should embody thesis, antithesis, and synthesis"),[4] which itself is based on Hegel's rationalization of the Trinity, it is unmistakable that *Ulysses* splits into three sections, the Telemachiad and the Homecoming themselves each comprising three chapters. (Ellmann seems to have acquired Augustine's habit of finding triads in apparently nonreligious contexts. "St. Augustine, having arrived at his Trinitarian idea of God, saw manifestations of this supernatural principle in all sorts of sheerly natural phenomena. Every triad, however secular, was for him another sign of the Trinity.")[5] The question becomes whether Joyce, in setting up various triads (for example, "the trinity of Stephen, Bloom, and Molly"[6] or Stephen, Bloom, and D. B. Murphy),[7] lays a secular trinitarian foundation for *Ulysses.* As we approach an answer, we do well to notice the outlandish (however analogical) reasoning that tends to support this idea. Ellmann suggests that "the cabman's horse, for his part, deposits a trinity of turds on the street in symbolic counterblow to the three-personed fusion in progress. (He also echoes Mulligan's trinity of eggs in *Telemachus*)."[8] To Father Boyle, "Stephen and Bloom, as Son and Father, unite not only in their symbolic urination but in their contemplation of each other in the light of Molly's mystery."[9] Is there not some oblivion in these observations to Joyce's parodic scatology, even though Ellmann and Boyle no doubt mean to be confronting it?

A more compelling approach is available for locating in *Ulysses* traces of Trinitarian theology. In *Beginnings,* Edward Said connects *"Authority"* to *"author,"* which he defines as "a person who originates or gives existence to something, a begetter, beginner, father, or ancestor, a person who sets forth written statements"[10]—a Father/father who begets the Word/word, if I may extrapolate. Evidence abounds that when Joyce (at least initially) adopted the role of artist-god he invoked the theology of the Trinity as a model. It is important to keep in mind that the Fathers' pandybat was Joyce's pen's next-of-kin, that Joyce's struggle against the Fathers always at first involves positioning himself within, in an effort eventually to coopt and in doing so subvert, their theology.

Cooptation of course can easily be read as cooperation. Catholic critics tend to believe that Joyce uses the Trinitarian Mystery as a foundation for his own generation of his word. Augustine is seen as the ultimate source of the analogy between the Word and Joyce's words since in Augustine the parturition of the Word is in turn based on the parturition of the poet's inner word—a justification for Joyce's appropriating what was literary in the first place.[11] Kenneth Burke (in *The Rhetoric of Religion*) generalizes the point: "Whereas the words for the 'supernatural' realm are necessarily borrowed from the realm of our everyday experiences . . . once a terminology has been developed for special theological purposes, the order can become reversed."[12] But in *Ulysses* it is not merely a matter of terminology: a conceptual order is being reversed. To convey the Mystery of God's generation of His Word, Augustine relies on the analogy of the poet's conception of the inner word. "The procession of the inner word or image from the poet's mind is . . . a kind of self-communication which may serve as a human analogue or exemplar to illustrate the divine processions since it suggests at least at another level the possibility of distinctness of persons within a perfectly unique consubstantiality of nature."[13] Conversely, the Mystery of God's generation of His Word serves analogically to convey the "mystery" of Joyce's conception of his words.

To penetrate the Mystery of the Trinity, Aquinas, like Augustine, appeals to analogies drawn from the operations of the human mind.[14] Throughout Aquinas's "Treatise on the Trinity," the procession of the Word is said to be analogous to an "act of Intellect." Aquinas prompts readers who seek to understand the manner in which the Son proceeds from the Father to ponder "an intelligible emanation, for example, of the intelligible word which proceeds from the speaker, yet remains in him. In that sense the Catholic Faith understands procession as existing in God" (*ST,* I, Q. 27, Art. 1).

The critic, then, who espouses, however epigrammatically, an analogy between the Word and Joyce's words draws on a tradition stretching back through the Scholastics to the Church Fathers. Despite all the textuality of Joyce's writing, all the "female excess," Joyce does project a keen sense of himself as an artist-god parturiating his words on the Trinitarian model; his heritage was distinctly patriarchal. Any conception of Joyce as a writer of *écriture féminine* would need to account for this genealogy.

But the analogy contains a snag: Aquinas compares the craftsman's word, and not his created object, to the Trinitarian Word. He teaches that "the craftsman works through the word conceived in his mind, and through the love of his will regarding some object. Hence also God the Father made the creature through His Word, which is His Son; and through His Love, which is the Holy Ghost" (*ST,* I, Q. 45, Art. 6). Aquinas avoids an analogy between the Son's procession from the Father and the making of an artistic product. He views "*generation,* whereby one proceeds from another as a son," as different from "*making,*" whereby "the maker makes something out of external matter, as a carpenter makes a bench out of wood." To Aquinas, God begets the Word from Himself, as "a man begets a son from himself"; but an artisan makes something out of material external to himself. The Son is therefore begotten not made (*ST*, I, Q. 41, Art. 3). If we were dealing with any writer besides Joyce, it might be wise to accept Aquinas's discrimination and let the matter drop: all artists are artisans (rather than Thomistic "begetters") to the extent that they create an art object out of material that is external to themselves. But Joyce invites us to pursue the analogy between God vis-à-vis His Word and the artist-god vis-à-vis his words, as those words constitute the artistic product *Ulysses*.

Aquinas states that "true *generation*" is exemplified in the procession of one from another as a son from a father (*ST*, I, Q. 41, Art. 3). Joyce, as if to satisfy this criterion, conceives of his work as his offspring. In a letter to Nora, he personifies *Dubliners* as "the child" he had been carrying; he describes himself feeding this "child" out of his brain and memory (*SL* 202–03). It is through the phallic Buck that Joyce indirectly depicts himself conceiving of *Ulysses* as his progeny. Mulligan calls out in "Scylla and Charybdis," "Wait. I am big with child. I have an unborn child in my brain." Mulligan's child is identified as art: he goes on to exclaim, "Pallas Athena! A play! The play's the thing! Let me parturiate!" (*U* 171). Not only is Buck on the verge of parturiating his own play, *Everyman His Own Wife or A Honeymoon in the Hand* (*U* 178), but he quotes significantly from *Hamlet;* his allusion to a self-reflexive line in *Hamlet* reflects on the self-reflexiveness at this moment of *Ulysses*.

Buck's parodic dramatization of the birth of the work of art in his brain ("He clasp[s] his paunchbrow with both birthaiding hands" [*U* 171]) is triggered by Stephen's refutation of Sabellius. Catching just the drift of Stephen's Shakespeare theories as they depend on the Trinitarian Mystery, Mulligan translates from theology to art. He finds in the Sabellian heresy that the Son is "Himself his own father" (*U* 171) inspiration to enact the trope that Joyce employs in his letters to define his relation to art: the artist begetting his work of art as his child. At least at this stage in the novel (through "Scylla and Charybdis"), Joyce seems caught up in the parturiating power of his pen; with it he will produce a "son."

This patriarchal idea of artistic conception, in fact, dies hard, for "Oxen of the Sun," a late chapter, is of course dedicated to the correlation of the processes of the birth of a son and the birth of language (no women writers are imitated). Not only does this episode present concurrently Mrs. Purefoy's bearing of her baby boy and the evolution of the English language, but toward the end of "Oxen," Joyce recreates the Nativity scene over which a "cloudburst pours its torrent . . . upon the utterance of the word" (*U* 345).

The sign of (divine) paternity, in Aquinas, is the beauty of the Son. His interests unsurprisingly more theological than aesthetic,[15] Aquinas takes up the issue of beauty in answering the question of "Whether the Essential Attributes Are Appropriated to the Persons [of the Trinity] in a Fitting Manner by the Holy Doctors?" (*ST*, I, Q. 39, Art. 8). The correct response (he informs us) is, in short, yes. Aquinas defends the attribution of *"eternity"* to the Father, *"species* to the Son, [and] *use* to the Holy Ghost." It is in explaining the appropriateness of assigning "species or beauty" to the Son that Aquinas proposes the criteria Stephen adopts in *A Portrait* as a test for all aesthetic objects. Aquinas expounds, one by one, the relation of each of the three qualities of beauty to the Son. The first, *"integrity* or *perfection,"* suits Him, since "He as Son has in Himself truly and perfectly the nature of the Father." The second, "due *proportion* or *harmony,"* "agrees with the Son's property . . . inasmuch as He is the express Image of the Father." And from this, it is interesting to note, Aquinas deduces that perfect representation, even of an ugly thing, creates a beautiful image—from which we might deduce that, if the theological equivalent to representation is the perfect harmony of Father and Son, a break with representation may imply repudiation of a Trinitarian idea of partriarchal production. The third criterion, *"brightness* or *clarity,"* "agrees with the property of the Son, as the Word, which is the light and splendor of the intellect." Quoting Augustine, Aquinas thus concludes that the Word is *"the art of the omnipotent God"* (*ST*, I, Q. 39, Art. 8). *"[W]holeness, harmony and radiance"* (*P* 212) not only serve as aesthetic criteria that in their structural neatness eliminate "female excess," but they spring up directly out of the theology of one of the most powerful philosophers of the Church.

That Aquinas saw beauty as an essential and fitting attribute of the Word reinforces the analogy between the Word and Joyce's words once the "beauty" of Joyce's language is granted. In order to be beautiful, in secularized Thomistic terms, Joyce's words would have to (1) possess integrity or perfection, that is, embody the nature of the father, who is, in the analogy, Joyce. And it is true that from its inception *Ulysses* has inspired critics to regard it as a formal correlative of Joyce's real life experience and psychosexual urges. (2) The novel would have to manifest due proportion or harmony, which is tantamount in Aquinas to representing things (including the ugly) perfectly. *Ulysses* has been taken—from Pound, through Harry Levin, to Hugh Kenner in *Dublin's Joyce*—as the quintessential naturalistic novel. Joyce fanatically wanted to rebuild Dublin exactly; so orange chamber pots became as indispensable as anything else. If Joyce's naturalism is based on the Thomistic model, of course, the *Ulysses* chamber pot as express image of real Dublin chamber pots is token of *Ulysses* itself as express image of Joyce. (3) The novel would have to radiate brightness or clarity, in other words, emit the light and splendor of the

intellect behind it. While it is aggressively naturalistic, in its
equally aggressive linguistic performativeness, *Ulysses* reflects
the brilliance of a supporting intelligence.

Joyce establishes an intimate bond between himself and his
book through the conspicuous self-referentiality of its language. The linguistic solipsism of *Ulysses*, which has been
taken as evidence of its alienation from a single originating
consciousness, (also) advertises the permeating presence of the
artist-god Joyce. Rather than pointing to the notion that
"writing seems to be divorced from the writer,"[16] or perhaps
I should say, paradoxically even as Joyce's linguistic designing
points to such ideas, it signals the imposition of the masterful
artist-god himself—the artist-god who secured his pen through
a trade-in of the pandybat. Said has asserted that "beginning
and beginning-again are historical whereas origins are divine;[17]
Joyce initially adopted a divine metaphor as his paradigm of
artistic production.

Even the ostensibly realistic passages of the novel can seem
as mimetic of Joyce's mind as they are of a world outside the
book. To take one preliminary example among hundreds, near
the onset of "Eumaeus," we read: "Discussing these and
kindred topics they [Stephen and Bloom] made a beeline across
the back of the Customhouse and passed under the Loop Line
bridge where a brazier of coke burning in front of a sentrybox
or something like one attracted their rather lagging footsteps"
(*U* 503). Despite the apparent verisimilitude of this passage,
the picture it transmits is somewhat of a mirage. The brazier
of coke burns probably not in front of a sentrybox but in
front of "something like one." Also antagonistic to realism is
the suggestion that a brazier of coke attracts Stephen's and
Bloom's "lagging footsteps." The consubstantial chains of
"b's" (as if to compose a literary equivalent of the "beeline"),
blends ("kindred," "across," "bridge," "brazier," "sentrybox," "attracted"), and liquids ("Loop Line," "rather lag-

ging") propel the centripetal (authorial) as least as much as the centrifugal (textual) trajectory of the description.[18]

Insofar as *Ulysses* is a verbal artifact in ways such as these, the case may be made that Joyce had as an initial goal—a hereditary compulsion—the generation, speaking Thomistically, of a book that would be consubstantial with himself. There is a sense in which Joyce's words exist as his "inner word," a sense in which Joyce and his writing achieve a kind of self-sufficiency in their self-communication similar to the Augustinian conception of the unique consubstantiality of poet and poet's inner word or image. The Trinitarian artistic paradigm may then support both Joyce's realism and antirealism, which is not so startling if we remember that Aquinas uses realism as a *metaphor of* the ideal proportion of Creator and Word.

The language of *Ulysses* seeks to establish its consubstantiality with the mind of its begetter—longs for a perfect concord, a perfect filial union, with its paternal origin—in diverse ways. Readers of *Ulysses* are now well aware that frequently a character thinks or utters something that, if Joyce had produced a psychologically conventional novel, could belong only to another character's consciousness. The "Fetter Lane passage" does not need to be rehearsed. But it might bear mentioning that such unrealistic consubstantiality of thought is not the rarity that critical attention to this one passage may once have implied, as this intermingling abounds. Many Joyce critics now have their own set of such anomalies; some of mine thematize authorial investment.

Stephen alone shares phrases with (for example) Bloom, the Reverend Hugh C. Love, even Gerty MacDowell. Besides being cognizant of Stephen's Shakespeare theories after they have been formulated in Bloom's absence, Bloom also oddly seems to contribute to the vocabulary that Stephen uses. One of his meditations in "Calypso," "Dander along all day. Might meet a robber or two. Well, meet him" (*U* 47), appears to provide an image for Stephen's speculations in "Scylla and Charybdis": "Every life is many days, day after day. We walk through ourselves, *meeting robbers,* ghosts, giants, old men, young men, wives, widows, brothers-in-love, but always meeting ourselves" (*U* 175, my emphasis). If we imagine Stephen's list to be a loose tallying of the cast of characters in *Ulysses,* Joyce virtually announces here that he confronts himself in his text; through Stephen, Joyce is after all propounding in "Scylla and Charybdis" the theory of the artist fathering himself. Such intratextuality implicates Joyce and thus enacts the metaphor of literary filiation articulated in "Scylla and Charybdis."

While talking with Mr. Deasy in "Nestor," Stephen thinks enigmatically, "May I trespass on your valuable space" (*U* 27); in "Wandering Rocks," the clergyman Hugh C. Love half-echoes Stephen in assuring Mr. Lambert that he "won't trespass on [his] valuable time" (*U* 190). (Whether or not these phrases are clichés of letters to the editor or of formal conversation, as Brendan O Hehir has suggested to me, divisions of space and time are thus overcome in the artist-god's consciousness.) Stephen famously uses the phrase "all in all" to describe both Shakespeare and God in "Scylla and Charybdis" (*U* 174, 175); Gerty, in "Nausicaa," adopts this same terminology in fantasizing about Bloom as he gazes fixedly at her on the beach. Exposing Gerty's emotions—in vocabulary that might be read as Gerty's, or at least Gerty's were she somewhat literary—the chapter reveals that "she would follow, her dream of love, the dictates of her heart that told her he was her all in all, the only man in all the world for her for love was the master guide" (*U* 299). Though obviously "all in all" is theological phraseology already romanced, Joyce's planting of the phrase in minds of clearly distinct sensibilities aligns him cleverly with the very God about whom Stephen uses the formulation.

Language annexes the minds of sundry characters to Stephen's mind; they all sacrifice autonomy in sharing words that parallactically reflect back on their source—Joyce. The reflection back is the point—the words must be merged into one Word in order to be united with the Creator. And that unity is accomplished only if linguistic conjoining takes place that fuses not merely the thoughts of two characters but also the thoughts of characters with the text itself—Bakhtinian narratological transgressions (in the spirit of Kenner's Uncle Charles Principle) that intimate and emblematize the consubstantiality of all consciousnesses in the book with their creator's. In "Scylla and Charybdis," John Eglinton says, "A shrew . . . is not a useful portal of discovery, one should imagine"; he says this "shrewdly" (*U* 156). Likewise, when the text reports Mr. Best's exclamation—"Piper! . . . Is Piper back?"—it reports that Mr. Best "piped" his words. "Piper! Mr Best piped. Is Piper back?" Mr. Best's words even catalyze a textual variation on "Peter Piper Picked a Peck of Pickled Peppers": after relaying Mr. Best's lines, *Ulysses* proceeds obsessively with "Peter Piper pecked a peck of pick of peck of pickled pepper" (*U* 157). Mr. Best and the text are clearly of one mind—Joyce's—here. So are Mr. Lyster and the text: "O, Father Dineen! Directly!" calls out Mr. Lyster to an attendant; then follows "Swiftly rectly creaking rectly rectly he was rectly gone" (*U* 173). And while it is one thing for the text to pick up on or fool with the words of the characters, it seems even more narratologically transgressive for a character to toy with the language of the text. In blurting out "Hoopsa!" in "Circe" (*U* 409), Zoe reiterates a motif of the beginning of "Oxen": "Hoopsa, boyaboy hoopsa!" (*U* 314). Especially in "Circe," there are no bounds to this sort of crossing over.

Analogies are tough to prove. They either strike a chord or they do not; and they are always imperfect. *Ulysses* invites us nonetheless to look at Augustinian/Thomistic Trinitarian theology for an analogy of its self-reflexivity of style: Stephen of course elaborates explicitly a metaphor of literary filiation, and *Joyce* thereby at least raises the issue of his overriding authority/authorship. To get to the crux of the matter, the fine distinction that Stephen, following the Catholic Church, wishes to maintain is that we may assert that the Father is consubstantial with the Son (this is how Stephen phrases the concept in "Scylla and Charybdis," as he interlaces it with his theory of Shakespeare: he describes Shakespeare ethereally as "a ghost, a shadow now, the wind by Elsinore's rocks or what you will, the sea's voice, a voice heard only in the heart of him who is the substance of his shadow, the son consubstantial with the father" [*U* 162]), but it is inaccurate to assert, with Sabellius, that "the Father was Himself His own Son." The idea of consubstantiality of the Father and the Son (which became orthodox at the Council of Nicea in A.D. 325) does indeed mean that "the Son [is] fully God, in the sense of sharing the same divine nature as His Father," that "the divine *ousia,* simple and indivisible, is shared at once by Father and Son." Yet—and here Catholic theologians pull back from Sabellius, to occupy a middle ground between him and Arius— the distinction between the two Persons is real, lying in the difference "between the Godhead considered as eternally activating, expressing and begetting Itself, and the selfsame Godhead considered as eternally activated, expressed and begotten. The Son is the selfsame Godhead as the Father, but that Godhead manifested rather than immanent" (*Christian Doctrines* 235, 247).

If we accept, as by now most critics have, Shechner's reading of Stephen's Shakespeare theory that "Shakespeare . . . is only the pretext . . . ; James Joyce is the text,"[19] taking into account that Stephen moves from the topic of Shakespeare's relation to his work to that of the relationship of the First and Second Persons of the Trinity, then we are compelled to find *in Joyce's* creativity an artistic analogue of the consubstantiality of Father and Son. It seems likely that Joyce wrote a self-conscious novel (not to be a forerunner in poststructuralist poetics but) because he had "the cursed jesuit strain in [him], only . . . injected the

wrong way" (*U* 7), and thus produced a literary equivalent
of the parturition of the Word—by begetting, expressing, and
activating the words of *Ulysses,* within which he brightly
manifested himself. The evidence I have presented up to this
point certainly suggests that the Father-Son relationship is the
theological-literary basis of *Ulysses.* But how stable is it?

II

*I think a child should be allowed to take his father's or
mother's name at will on coming of age. Paternity is a
legal fiction.*
—Joyce, *Selected Letters*

Even as the self-conscious, the antinarrative features of *Ulysses*—perhaps most prominently, the newspaper headlines of
"Aeolus," the blatant recombinations of words in "Sirens,"
the lists of (especially) "Cyclops," the catechism format of
"Ithaca," "Penelope" in general, the pervasive neologisms and
puns—advertise Joyce's presence in his writing, his consubstantiality with his words, they are precisely what ruptures
the book's representationalism and narrative line. One means
by which Joyce constructs a literary analogue of the Trinitarian
Mystery turns out to be the same means by which he destroys
the fathers'/Fathers' mode of writing—not to mention their
theology, by again making light of it—and procures for himself
a bit of fun. Joyce plants tiny linguistic explosives, agents of
disintegration, within the very material that upholds the parallel between God-the-Father and His Word and Joyce and
his words, a move that is consonant with his repudiation of
naturalism as, analogically speaking, sensualist and sadistic—
perhaps sadistic in the sense of violently mastering reality.
The very linguistic networks I use in this chapter as examples
of Joyce's authorial presence (even as they make the point of
his presence) set off self-motivated signifying chains. Once
"activated, expressed, and begotten," the paternally produced
words, in filial rebellion, dart off on their own trajectories.

Joyce dramatizes the point. When Stephen, toward the end of "Oxen," in his role as "lord" blurts out "Burke's!" (*U* 345) (the climactic enunciation the whole chapter had been building up to), the Trinitarian Word splinters from a divine utterance into the chapter's final pages of fragments of modern slang, a polyglot of modern speech, or, in other words, into MacCabe's signifier(s) "in excess of a signified, a name in excess of its bearer: the Name of the Father" (MacCabe 129). Joyce gets to the logos (but) in the process of shattering the Logos. Once the heterogeneous linguistic terrain has been opened up, there is no turning back; the Logos fizzles out to the point that it cannot be recuperated. The Church Joyce was rebelling against was not elastic enough to make the transition back from an Irish pub to the Second Person of the Trinity. One could of course argue, as Beryl Schlossman does in *Joyce's Catholic Comedy of Language,* that (in brief) Joyce textualizes Catholicism and thus retains it in a new form, but even her position attributes to Joyce belief in the sacred, in Trinitarian Mystery with its emphasis on Paternity and Filiation—which I believe Joyce wished to disavow, even if his disavowal necessitates a precedent avowal, to demystify without remystifying in the process. Though it is crucial that Stephen comes up with his Shakespeare/Trinitarian aesthetic theory, it is equally crucial to notice his rejection of it.

"God-the-Father" is no more recuperable than the Logos. Once author-god produces a Text that in turn reflects (is consubstantial with) him, he too becomes textualized, unidentifiable, indefinable. As Stephen (also) says, "Paternity may be a legal fiction" (*U* 170): "the artist weave[s] and [then] unweave[s] his image" (*U* 159) in the form of his text/*textus*/tapestry. Joyce finally may be located, if at all, in "the play of possibilities produced by the various discourses of the text" (MacCabe 68). Joyce was compelled to kill off the author-god in himself because this self-image was initially so insistent.

But perhaps I should have written that "the artist weave[s] and [then] unweave[s] his [her?] image" in the form of *her* text/*textus*/tapestry, since it is for the most part women who weave tapestries ("As we, or mother Dana, weave and unweave our bodies, Stephen said" [*U* 159]) and Penelope who wove one to preserve herself from men. Inasmuch as Joyce becomes synonymous with his Text, and inasmuch as his Text is a tapestry (a fair metaphor I think with respect to a novel that ends with "Penelope"), has not Joyce again attempted to assume the feminine position? Is not the relinquishing of his authorial signature part of exactly such a shift? Artist-god produces a Son/Word/words that turn out to be a Text that turns out to be a piece of linguistic embroidery woven by a woman. In fact, when Joyce in his letter to Nora imagined *Dubliners* as his offspring, he was comparing his fictional parturition with hers from her womb: he wrote of "the child which [he had] carried for years and years in the womb of the imagination as [Nora] carried in [her] womb the children [she loved]" (*SL* 202–03). And, just as it is Mary's blessed body that bears the "Son" in the Bible, it is Mina Purefoy's female body that bears the "son" in "Oxen." (We might have expected that Buck's onanistic parturition would not ultimately command Joyce's loyalty.) Joyce slides slowly in the course of *Ulysses* from one artistic trope to another: from God's parturition of the Word to a woman's, perhaps Mary's (especially given Mina Purefoy's identity as postfiguration of the Virgin), parturition of the word/words from the womb.

III

Thou shalt not make thee any graven image, or any likeness of any thing that is in heaven above, or that is in the earth beneath, or that is in the waters beneath the earth.
—Deuteronomy 5:8

A worshipper of the Scarlet Woman.
—Alexander J. Dowie, "Circe"

At this point my argument takes a turn, a temporal swerving back, a spatial crossing of the Atlantic Ocean, as well as somewhat of a turn against itself. We now remove ourselves to nineteenth-century America for a glance at Nathaniel Hawthorne, who aligns Catholicism and wordplay while nervously trying to steer clear of both. A foil for Joyce, Hawthorne seems to suggest that there *is* something distinctively Catholic not only in Joyce's self-investment in his text but in his production of self-conscious writing. Invoking Hawthorne and, through him, briefly, Protestant poetics also enables us to see the strong literary-historical sense of kinship between the use of language for its own sake and fetishism, which, according to a traditional Protestant criticism, bears its own connection to Catholicism. Hence a key question is raised: Just how subversive is Joyce's emptying out of Catholic theology, his glorifying of the linguistic symbol over the thing symbolized, given that his means of evacuating Catholic theology and hence his persistent weapon against the Church, linguistic excess, turns out to have its own attachment to the Church?

Grappling with one anxiety Joyce was not plagued with, Hawthorne certainly worries over his Puritan ancestors' lack of respect for the artist. In "The Custom-House," he dramatizes the disdainful view they would have had of him had they known of his creative writing: " 'What is he?' murmurs one gray shadow of my forefathers to the other. 'A writer of story-books! What kind of a business in life,—what mode of glorifying God, or being serviceable to mankind in his day and generation,—may that be? Why, the degenerate fellow might as well have been a fiddler!' "[20] Unlike Thomas Aquinas, Hawthorne's Puritan forefathers perceived and promoted no happy parallel between the human creation of a work of art and God's creation of the Word or world. To them such a parallel was unthinkable.

Although Hawthorne distinguished himself from his fiction-hating fathers by becoming a fiction writer, he admits that he inherited some of their propensities: "Let them scorn me as they will, strong traits of their nature have intertwined themselves with mine" (*SL* 10). Hawthorne seems particularly fearful of appearing to enter his fictional construct in a way that might resemble God's self-investment in the world. In "The Custom-House," he lays down strictures that seem designed to preclude the descent of the artist into his creation. First of all, this preface begins with Hawthorne's criticism of authorial indulgence in "confidential depths of revelation as could fittingly be addressed, only and exclusively, to the one heart and mind of perfect sympathy" (*SL* 3). An author must not be too personal. Autobiography itself is justified only when, to create a relation with his audience, the author imagines "that a friend, a kind and apprehensive, though not the closest friend, is listening to [his] talk," and not when the author's "inmost Me" is exposed from "behind its veil" (*SL* 4). (Joyce of course went off scandalously in the opposite autobiographical direction.) "It is scarcely decorous," Hawthorne remarks astringently, "to speak all, even where we speak impersonally" (*SL* 4). Wholeness (one must not speak "all," one must not rival God) is stigmatized. Second, Hawthorne's insistence that "the main facts" of the story of *The Scarlet Letter* are "authorized and authenticated by the document of Mr. Surveyor Pue" (*SL* 32) and his need to feign for himself a "true position as editor" (*SL* 4) show his typical Puritan impulse to distance himself from a creative role. While Joyce attempts literarily to pull the rug out from under Trinitarian theology, a Catholic Mystery he gets a huge amount of productivity out of in the first place, no such theological metaphor of artistic production was available to Hawthorne either to preserve artistically or to undermine.

Given Hawthorne's reluctance to be located in his writing, his reluctance to play the role of God-the-Father generating the Word/words, we should not expect to find in his works self-conscious linguistic patterns that would call attention to his authorial designing. And it is the case that Hawthorne does not fetishize language. The few instances of what look like Joycean play that do turn up are either inadvertent or subliminally functional.

In "The Custom-House," for instance, Hawthorne uses the term "custom" and terms that contain the word "custom," which were they employed by Joyce would serve the purpose of establishing, and then disseminating, his playful presence in the text. Hawthorne writes of his fellow workers: "They spent a good deal of time . . . asleep in their accustomed corners, with their chairs tilted back against the wall" (*SL* 14). Speaking later (also in "The Custom-House") about the Collector, he explains that "it was only with the assistance of a servant . . . that he could slowly and painfully ascend the Custom-House steps, and, with a toilsome progress across the floor, attain his customary chair beside the fireplace" (*SL* 20). At the beginning of chapter 23, Hawthorne sustains his custom-house wordplay, again perhaps unwittingly, by writing that military music "denoted the advance of the procession of magistrates and citizens, on its way towards the meeting-*house;* where, in compliance with a *custom* thus early established, and ever since observed, the Reverend Mr. Dimmesdale was to deliver an Election Sermon" (*SL* 236, my emphases). But the apparently ludic language in all three of these examples (a nice contrast with Joyce's self-conscious "Customhouse" passage), as well as the network of language that, because of the unifying word "Custom-House," is comprised by the terms "accustomed," "customary," "meeting-house," and "custom," is a function of Hawthorne's descriptive tact rather than his playful self-expression.

The wordplay that Hawthorne permits himself tends to promote meaning at the narrative level and thus underlines his refusal to use language for its own sake. The pun on "election," for instance, in Dimmesdale's "Election Sermon" is not a pun for pun's sake (if it is a pun at all). Since the elected governor had to be, in the Puritan view, a member of the Elect, the two meanings of the pun complement each other in ways that enhance, if not constitute, the story line. The pun implicit in Bellingham's judgment that Dimmesdale must "inevitably fall" refers to the possibility of Dimmesdale's physical fall in order to comment on his spiritually fallen state: "Bellingham, for the last few moments, had kept an anxious eye upon [Dimmesdale]. He now left his own place in the procession, and advanced to give assistance; judging from Mr. Dimmesdale's aspect that he must otherwise inevitably fall" (*SL* 252). Dimmesdale's physical fall, had he taken it, would hardly have mattered compared to what such an act would have signified spiritually; that he does not even literally take a plunge clinches the point, highlighting that the issue is whether he is irredeemably fallen. Hawthorne's play with words such as "chill," "chills," and "chilliness" to comment on Chillingworth and "dimmest of all shadows" and "dimmer" to comment on Dimmesdale brings out the allegorical—the functional—nature of Hawthorne's characters, making us feel as if we were back in Bunyan's *Pilgrim's Progress* (or for that matter in the world of some of Hawthorne's own short stories), where name defines character. The Hawthornean pun does not point metalinguistically to language but allegorically to spiritual truths.

Such allegorizing seems to bear its own relationship to (a Marxist conception of) fetishism, as Simpson shows in his reading of Dickens, and it may be that Hawthorne is participating in the fetishism of allegory. (I doubt that he is condemning it, by situating "the figurative ingenuity of his writing as the image of a world . . . disconnected and alienated," as Simpson believes Dickens does.)[21] But in any case Hawthorne avoids fetishizing language. There was, in the nineteenth century, an articulated Protestant antipathy to such a practice. Simpson explains that the famous argument against "poetic diction" belongs in the context of [the] case against ornament. As Wordsworth describes it, it is poetic diction that (like the London theaters) offers an image divorced from a reality, tempting us by its surface coruscations to exercise on language alone the powers that properly belong to the feelings and passions. Like the fetish, such improper language seeks to inhibit the reference back from sign to signifying act; and, like the fetish, the more ornamental and decorative it is (the more tricks, enigmas, and hieroglyphs it employs), the less we suspect any authentic origin in the powers within.[22]

Though he certainly seems to be tempted to spin out such linguistic embroidery, Hawthorne restrains himself.

Resisting the impulse to use self-conscious language that might point to a designing artist-god behind it and thus invoke the parallel with the Trinitarian generation of the Word, Hawthorne escapes participating in the purported Catholic obsession with language that inhibits the "reference back from sign to signifying act" (a risk that, as R. Howard Bloch shows, medieval theologians *were* willing to run, despite the "danger of woman" held in language). Instead Hawthorne makes a point of the impoverishment of his words vis-à-vis the Word. Although Hester describes the Reverend Dimmesdale as "a learned and pious minister of the Word" (*SL* 242), the power of his Election Sermon is staggering because of its ability to surpass language. Hester Prynne, though barely able to hear the words of the speech, listens with "intentness," sympathizes "intimately," so that the speech has "throughout a meaning for her, entirely apart from its indistinguishable words." Had they been more distinctly audible, the words, being "a grosser medium, [might] have clogged the spiritual sense." The shifting tones of the speech are sufficient to "envelop" Hester "with an atmosphere of awe and solemn grandeur" (*SL* 243). Upon hearing the final word, "the multitude, silent till then, broke out in a strange, deep voice of awe and wonder, which could not as yet find utterance, save in this murmur that rolled so heavily after the departed spirit" (*SL* 257). Dimmesdale has rendered this multitude speechless. The "learned and pious minister of the Word" preaches best when words are transcended. The Word exceeds banal words; a parallel would only demean God.

Yet despite Hawthorne's efforts to deflect attention away from any reinforcing he might do of a Word/word analogy, Tony Tanner in *City of Words* manages to find in the scarlet letter itself at least an early indication in American literature of a preoccupation with writing *in se*. "The very title *The Scarlet Letter* suggests that the subject will be involved with a matter of language, alphabetical if not lexical, and the skilful needlework which Hester Prynne expended on her scarlet letter 'A' may be compared to the creative care Hawthorne lavishes on the letters which make up his book."[23] Tanner has shrewdly identified the "A" as a linguistic sign, but he has overlooked its Catholicity. Not only do the colors of the "fine red cloth" and "gold embroidery" of the letter link it with stained glass, but it is described in terms that call to mind an artistic Catholic embellishment, certainly like those of which Protestants disapproved. By the "forgotten art" of embroidery, Hester creates "an ornamental article of dress" (*SL* 31), a "spiritual adornment" (*SL* 81–82) that is "artistically done" (*SL* 53) and that to the speaker of "The Custom-House" has the status of "a most curious relic" (*SL* 33). It is of course this extravagant work of art that the Puritans of the novel pin on Hester and refuse to interpret in any other way than as an insignia of her "stain," her sin. Catholic ornamentation, which Protestants decried as fetishistic, appropriately becomes synonymous in Hawthorne's novel with the first letter of the alphabet, with a basic constituent of writing, as if to indicate sin in linguistic self-reflexivity. The degree to which Hawthorne's writing of the novel is tantamount to Hester's embroidery of the "A"

equals the degree to which he is in danger of following a
Catholic poetics promoting embellishment, in particular, the
frills of word games dissociated from narrative. At the very
least, we can say that Hawthorne acknowledges a tie between
the Catholic Church and self-conscious language.

In this he was not alone. As Simpson points out, writers in
the Protestant tradition criticized Catholicism for its love of
objects and words. While Puritans may have participated,
through their love of allegory, in a fetishism of the signified,
they opposed Catholic fetishism of the signifier.

> Carlyle wrote of the Puritans as "men intent on the real
> essence of things" engaged in a struggle against "men intent
> on the semblances and forms of things." Coleridge accused
> Catholicism of encouraging attention to "refracted and
> distorted truths, profound ideas sensualized into idols, or
> at the lowest rate lofty and affecting imaginations, safe while
> they remained general and indefinite, but debased and ren-
> dered noxious by their application in detail." . . . Locke
> also had decided that Catholics were idolaters, idolatry
> being defined as "performing outward worship . . . before
> an image, where either the place, time, or other circum-
> stances give the spectator reason to presume that one is
> employed in some act of religious or divine worship." And,
> in a sonnet on the revival of Popery composed as part of
> a sequence retelling centuries of English history, Words-
> worth speaks of the people again embracing their "Gods
> of wood and stone."[24]

Wood and stone are commensurate with ink and paper if the
words produced cease to represent things and "are so far from
carrying the mind on to any farther contemplation, that they
rather invite it to stop at them alone; forming, as it were, a
specious kind of skreen between us and nature."[25]

Considering the Protestant attack on both religious and poetic ornamentation as well as the correlation Protestants made

between such empty forms and Catholicism, one has to wonder whether Joyce, oddly enough by virtue of his translation of the Logos to logos, did not end up extending rather than sabotaging the religion of the Fathers. While Hawthorne pinned "the scarlet letter" on Hester, Joyce uses it to embroider his Text/tapestry. And yet, in acknowledging the intensity and authenticity of Joyce's rebellion against the Fathers, we must ask whether Joyce does not in some way capitalize on his propensity to fetishize language *and* still manage to escape rather than expand Catholic patriarchy. The Barthesian Text, the text of embroidery, arrives at Catholicism in the ways I have just described; but the embroiderers turn out to be women, Hester and Molly/Penelope, even Mary. (Medieval misogynists were not the only ones who felt the presence of "woman" in language. Naomi Schor's hypothesis that excessive detail and ornamentation are "feminine" is vindicated in both Hawthorne and Joyce.) Just as the Word splinters into Joyce's words, and Wordplay becomes wordplay, what is effected under the aegis of Father-Son consubstantiality seems finally to be claimed or taken over by femininity. Joyce's parturition of the Word/words, which sets up the Trinitarian analogy, in the end seems imaginable only as birth from, or even within, the womb. (Like Bloom, who gives birth in the course of *Ulysses,* Joyce appears to have a craving for a womb of his own.) *Ulysses,* then, seems to suggest that the Protestant charges against Catholicism of Mariolatry and ornamental linguistic fetishism are true and related. Paradoxically, Joyce's rebellion against the stern Fathers of the Church results in, just what was denigrated by Protestants, Catholic worship of art and motherhood. In this way Catholicism arrives at Catholicism, but this is not to deny that Joyce's rebellion has an object, or that that object lurks within the Church.

5

"Petticoat Government"

I

Nora began to buy her hats from
Agnès, the fashionable milliner, and
her dresses from Helen's skillful
dressmaker. Joyce approved this new
interest; as he grew older, women
more and more seemed to him dolls,
unfortunately not mindless, to be got
up as prettily as possible. In a burst
of impatience he told Stuart Gilbert,
"La femme c'est rien." When Frank
Budgen protested, in the midst of one
of Joyce's now frequent diatribes
against women, that in the old days
he had at least thought their bodies
desirable and provoking, Joyce retort-
ed, "Macchè! Perhaps I did. But now
I don't care a damn about their bod-
ies. I am only interested in their
clothes." The bills from Agnès and
others that came in to gratify this in-
terest did not dismay him.
—Ellmann, *James Joyce*

124

Joyce works through Catholicism to flee it; and insofar as he grounds his rebellion in the very object he lashes out against, he reveals his paradoxical investment in what he wished to escape. To say he "blows up" the Church would be an apt way of capturing the duplicity of his strategy, except that the image lacks the subtlety of Joyce's moves. If Joyce's preoccupation with language per se bears an analogical relation to the Catholic love of art and ornamentation, then that aspect of Catholicism too is magnified, especially as Joyce yields what becomes in the efflorescence of *Ulysses* his increasingly playful pen to Molly Bloom, who raises drastically the degree of linguistic pleasure in/of the Text. But if Joyce's wordplay begins as merely an analogue of Catholic ornamentation, it does not end there. It constitutes the most radical component of a master plan—whose mistress is Molly—designed to situate Joyce to fly by Stephen's nets, to turn the law of the fathers/Fathers on its head.

This "master plan," as I call it, had a nineteenth-century historical/psychological precedent. It is in the spirit of Leopold von Sacher-Masoch's masochism that Joyce appropriated opportunistically the enemy's weapon. By masochism, then, I am referring to the Deleuzean paradigm as laid out in *Masochism: An Interpretation of Coldness and Cruelty,* based directly on the writing of Masoch. Gilles Deleuze draws his theory straight from the eponymous source, from the writer after whom Krafft-Ebing named masochism. And Joyce knew—as we shall see, lived—Masoch. Application of Deleuze's conception of masochism to Joyce is further justified in that Deleuze urges students of masochism to take a literary approach, since the original definitions of sadism and masochism stem from literature: "The clinical specificities of sadism and masochism are not separable from the literary values peculiar to Sade and Masoch."[1] Deleuze argues for a "genuinely formal, almost deductive psychoanalysis which would attend first of all to the formal patterns underlying [sadism and masochism], viewed as formal elements of fictional art" (*M* 65). My reading of masochism in Joyce will extend Deleuze's emphasis on the conjunction of this psychic phenomenon and formal artistic elements; from art masochism arose, and to art it will herein return. But to bolster my claim that Joyce's rebellion against the Church took the form of literary masochism, I want to make a prima facie case that Joyce was personally a masochist. So we must at this point descend from the esoterica of theology and its effects to the netherworld of pathology and perversions—from sacrament to sacrilege.

Masochism is based on the paradox that "the victim speaks the language of the torturer he is to himself" (*M* 17): "The masochistic hero appears to be educated and fashioned by the authoritarian woman whereas basically it is he who forms her, dresses her for the part and prompts the harsh words she addresses to him" (*M* 21). The victim adorns and educates his torturess; she in turn is his mouthpiece. Severin, the hero-masochist in Masoch's *Venus in Furs,* has the impulse at the onset of his lovelife with Wanda (his Venus) to "put her in furs. . . . Surely nothing could suit her better than regal fur!" (*VF* 136). Following in Severin's footsteps, Joyce attempted to transform Nora into a Venus in Furs. Though penniless at the time, he told Nora that he hoped to bring her "a splendid set of sable furs, cap, stole, and muff" (*SL* 172), which later became a "a grey squirrel cap with violets at the side and a long broad flat stole of grey squirrel and a beige granny muff of the same on a steel chain, both lined with violet satin" (*SL* 176).[2] Such symptoms of masochism fill Joyce's letters to his Venus.

As early as July 12, 1904, Joyce wrote to Nora, whom he addresses as "My dear little Goodie-Brown Shoes," that her "glove lay beside [him] all night." This might have seemed merely romantic, except that he elaborates on the glove's demeanor and state of dishabille: it was "unbuttoned—but otherwise conducted itself very properly" (*SL* 22). Joyce appears to have a glove fetish. Its manifestation marks the first moments of his budding relationship with Nora. Five years later Joyce makes explicit that gloves are to him a metaphor for Nora's private parts: "I hope you got my little present of gloves safely. . . . The nicest pair is that one of reindeer skin: it is lined with its own skin, simply turned inside out and should be warm, nearly as warm as certain districts of your body, Butterfly" (*SL* 176).

On November 19, 1904, Joyce finishes off a letter to Stanislaus with: "I really can't write. Nora is trying on a pair of drawers at the wardrobe Excuse me Jim" (*SL* 44). Joyce's drawers fetish reveals itself: "I wish you would wear black underclothes," he urges Nora. "I wish you would study how to please me, to provoke my desire of you. And you will, dearest, and we will be happy now, I feel" (*SL* 170). It may be that women's underwear was Joyce's pet fetish; especially a frilly pair seems to have roused him. "I wish you had a great store of all kinds of underclothes, in all delicate shades, stored away in a great perfumed press" (*SL* 180), he laments to Nora. When he finds out that she is actually going without any underwear at all, his imagination goes wild:

> Enough about moncy. I will send you a little banknote and hope you may be able to buy a pretty frilly pair of drawers at least for yourself out of it and will send you more when I am paid again. I would like you to wear drawers with three or four frills one over the other at the knees and up the thighs and great crimson bows in them, I mean not schoolgirls' drawers with a thin shabby lace border, tight round the legs and so thin that the flesh shows between them but women's (or if you prefer the word) ladies' drawers with a full loose bottom and wide legs, all frills and lace and ribbons, and heavy with perfume so that whenever

you show them, whether in pulling up your clothes hastily to do something or in cuddling yourself up prettily to be blocked, I can see only a swelling mass of white stuff and frills. . . . [*SL* 183–84]

As my ellipsis is meant to indicate, there is more, which readers may pursue at their discretion.

Nora's breasts were, as one might have anticipated, further objects of Joyce's fixation. The trouble was that they were too girlish. Joyce mocked them: "I am laughing at this moment as I think of those little girl's breasts of yours. You are a ridiculous person, Nora! Remember you are now twenty-four and your eldest child is four. Damn it, Nora, you must try to live up to your reputation and cease to be the little curious Galway girl you are and become a full happy loving woman" (*SL* 170). (Life imitates art. Wanda at the outset of *Venus in Furs* is "twenty-four at the most" [*VF* 127], and the first woman to make sexual overtures to Severin is a "charming chambermaid" [*VF* 145].) The cure was cocoa. Joyce mailed to Nora "enormous bags of shell cocoa" (*SL* 160) so that she would get "a *little* fatter on it." "I suppose you know why I hope that" (*SL* 166), Joyce half-kids her.

Perhaps the best evidence that he participated in Masoch's own variety of masochism is Joyce's craving to feel the sting of the lash of Nora's whip. (Masoch spent a lifetime exhorting his lovers to whip him.) On September 2, 1909, Joyce writes: "Nora, my 'true love', you must really take me in hand. Why have you allowed me to get into this state? Will you, dearest, take me as I am with my sins and follies and shelter me from misery. If you do not I feel my life will go to pieces. Tonight I have an idea madder than usual. I feel I would like to be flogged by you. I would like to see your eyes blazing with anger" (*SL* 166). A month and a half later, he receives a letter from Nora apparently chastising him for "how bad" he has been to her, to which he reacts in the downcast, excessively humble mood of a masochist: "All day, since I read your letter this morning, I have felt like a mongrel dog that has received a lash across the eyes. I have been awake now for two whole days and I wandered about the streets like some filthy cur whose mistress had cut him with her whip and hunted him from her door." Joyce describes her writing as that of a "queen" and conceives of himself as "a vile beast" (*SL* 177).

Another month passes and Joyce pleads for a literal whipping:

> I would be delighted to feel my flesh tingling under your hand. Do you know what I mean, Nora dear? I wish you would smack me or flog me even. Not in play, dear, in earnest and on my naked flesh. I wish you were strong, *strong*, dear, and had a big full proud bosom and big fat thighs. I would love to be whipped by you, Nora love! I would love to have done something to displease you, something trivial even, perhaps one of my rather dirty habits that make you laugh: and then to hear you call me into your room and then to find you sitting in an armchair with your fat thighs far apart and your face deep red with anger and a cane in your hand. To see you point to what I had done and then with a movement of rage pull me towards you and throw me face downwards across your lap. Then to feel your hands tearing down my trousers and inside clothes and turning up my shirt, to be struggling in your strong arms and in your lap, to feel you bending down (like an angry nurse whipping a child's bottom) until your big full bubbies almost touched me and to feel you flog, flog, flog me viciously on my naked quivering flesh!! (*SL* 188–89)

The glamorous furs, gloves, underwear (especially black), breasts (especially plump), and the whip/cane itself are all typical fetishes surrogate penises, possessed by Masoch's Venus in Furs—whose psychological effect is to alleviate the

victim's castration anxiety. "The main objects of fetishism in
Masoch's life and work are furs, shoes, the whip, the strange
helmets that he liked to adorn women with, or the various
disguises such as we find in *Venus*" (*M* 30). The fetish is the
means by which the masochist denies that a woman *lacks* a
penis, and thus it keeps him from having to face a menacing
reality. (I give here Freud's explanation since Deleuze incorporates it into his theory in *Masochism*.)[3] The process of disavowal central to masochism is "linked to castration not con-
tingently but essentially and originally; the expression of
fetishistic disavowal, 'No, the mother does not lack a phallus,'
is not one particular form of disavowal among others, but
formulates the very principle from which the other manifestations of disavowal derive" (*M* 110). (This position is obviously in marked contrast to the one Deleuze takes in *Anti-
Oedipus,* where he complains that "We have not finished
chanting the litany of the ignorances of the unconscious; it
knows nothing of castration or Oedipus, just as it knows
nothing of parents, gods, the law, lack.")[4]

   Joyce's letters to Nora seem to indicate that he needed such
fetishistic assistance in disavowing a menacing reality. It is
uncannily as if the flogging fathers/Fathers of *Dubliners* and
A Portrait have been replaced by Nora: Joyce's excitement in
imagining Nora's tearing down his trousers seems to cancel
out Stephen's anxiety in *A Portrait* over the question of who
lets down the boy's trousers, "the master or the boy himself"
(*P* 45). Joyce has not lost his fascination with flagellation.
Unwilling to receive the stick, pandybat, or whip from the
fathers/Fathers, he begs for it from his lover, a clear mother-
figure: "I am your child as I told you [Joyce wrote to Nora]
and you must be severe with me, my little mother. Punish me
as much as you like" (*SL* 188). And in that process of exchange, mastery that was impossible for him to possess in the
patriarchal world could be achieved. As Deleuze explains, "the

coldness of the stern mother is in reality a transmutation of cruelty from which the new man emerges" (*M* 11).

In his art, as in his life, Joyce produced images of Venus in Furs. (I take the art to reflect and extend—rather than to prove, since biographical clues abound—the masochism of Joyce's sexual desires. His obsessions cross promiscuously boundaries between fiction and life.) His "attempt at the sentimental education of a dark lady," as Ellmann calls *Giacomo Joyce*, begins with: "Who? A pale face surrounded by heavy odorous furs."[5] This unnamed Venus in Furs typically wears furs to keep herself warm in the "wintry air in the castle." She is further adorned with "tapping clacking heels" (*GJ* 1) and has "braided and pinnacled hair" (hair being another masochistic fetish) (*GJ* 12). "[A]s she walks a dark coil of her hair slowly uncoils and falls. Slowly uncoiling, falling hair" (*GJ* 11). The atmosphere of the castle seems merely to generate her acridity: she greets the narrator "wintrily and passes up the staircase darting at [him] for an instant out of her sluggish sidelong eyes a jet of liquorish venom" (*GJ* 15). She metamorphoses (as prefigured by her coils of hair) appropriately into a snake: "A starry snake has kissed me: a cold nightsnake. I am lost!" (*GJ* 15).

In *Ulysses,* cruel but sweet Gerty MacDowell aspires to fit the mold: "There was an innate refinement, a languid queenly *hauteur* about Gerty which was unmistakably evidenced in her delicate hands and higharched instep"; "Gerty's crowning glory was her wealth of wonderful hair [that] . . . nestled about her pretty head in a profusion of luxuriant clusters" (*U* 286); "Her shoes were the newest thing in footwear . . . with patent toecaps and just one smart buckle over her higharched instep"; "her shapely limbs [were] encased in finespun hose with highspliced heels and wide garter tops. As for undies they were Gerty's chief care" (*U* 287–88). She imagines herself at her wedding (that is "not to be") "wearing a sumptuous confection of grey trimmed with expensive blue fox" (*U* 288). Because Jacky and Tommy, the "exasperating little brats of twins," quarrel and generally act up, Gerty thinks that "someone ought to take them and give them a good hiding" (*U* 294). By swinging her buckled shoe and showing her "nainsook knickers" (*U* 300), "Gerty in Furs" brings Leopold Bloom, namesake of Sacher-Masoch, to a masturbatory climax in "Nausicaa," where musings on Molly and Blazes Boylan consummating their relationship—"O, he did. Into her. She did. Done. / Ah! / Mr Bloom with careful hand recomposed his wet shirt" (*U* 303)—well up in his consciousness immediately after his private fireworks, thus italicizing the masochistic nature of Bloom's sexual pleasure on the beach.

But I should note parenthetically that at the last moment Gerty's inadequacy is exposed. She has a limp, which we might feel justified reading as a sexual symbol since Joyce, through his description of Bloom's deflated organ as a "little limping devil" (*U* 303), implies a failed phallicism in Gerty's handicap. As if to explain that she is not sufficiently phallic to offer him full freedom from anxiety, Bloom remarks, "Glad I didn't know it when she was on show." He then confirms the point that he enjoyed her in psychological relation to his own masculinity, for which he needs compensation, by calling her a "hot little devil all the same" (*U* 301). Bloom needed Gerty to tease him, to punish him with her distance; had he known of her own symbolically castrated state, she could not have assisted him in fending off his. But he was spared; and so he is glad that he "didn't do it in the bath this morning over [Martha's] silly I will punish you letter" (*U* 301). Bloom clearly seeks punishment from women with power (over him). (As does Gabriel Conroy in "The Dead," whose dull lust "glow[s] angrily in his veins" as soon as he hears about Gretta's preoccupation with Michael Furey [*D* 218–19]. Once Gretta is distant, inaccessible—a figure framed by Gabriel's imaginary portrait *Distant Music*—she becomes, through mediation, desirable.)

In "Circe," the Venus in Furs figure multiplies. Bloom has craved and hence undergoes degrading cruelty at the hands of various "phallic women": Mrs. Yelverton Barry, Mrs. Bellingham, Mrs. Mervyn Talboys, Circe or Bella/Bello, and Molly, among others. Mrs. Barry, "in . . . *ivory gloves, wearing a sabletrimmed brickquilted dolman,*" charges that Bloom wrote her a letter "signed James Lovebirch. He said that he had seen from the gods my peerless globes as I sat in a box of the *Theatre Royal.* . . . He offered to send me . . . a work of fiction by Monsieur Paul de Kock, entitled *The Girl with the Three Pairs of Stays*" (*U* 379–80). Wearing a *"cap and seal coney mantle"* and carrying a *"huge opossum muff,"* Mrs. Bellingham complains that Bloom addressed her "in several handwritings with fulsome compliments as a Venus in furs" (*U* 380). And when the Honorable Mrs. Mervyn Talboys *"stamps her jingling spurs"* and threatens to "scourge the pigeonlivered cur as long as [she] can stand over him" and to "flay him alive, Bloom *"quails expectantly . . . pants cringing"* and admits "I love the danger" (*U* 381). (He later tells the FAN being held by Bella, "Enormously I desiderate your domination," after the FAN proclaims, "And the missus is master. Petticoat government" [*U* 430].) All three ladies testify that Bloom implored them "to chastise him as he richly deserves, to bestride and ride him, to give him a most vicious horsewhipping" (*U* 381). Bloom concedes that he "meant only the spanking idea. A warm tingling glow without effusion. Refined birching to stimulate the circulation" (*U* 382).

In scenes of graphic masochistic theatricality, Bloom becomes Bella/Bello's (Bloom and Bella trade sexes) "bondslave" (*U* 433): inflicting "heel discipline" Bella/Bello grinds her/his heel into Bloom's neck; she/he grabs Bloom's hair violently and drags him/her forward; she/he slaps and squats on Bloom's

face; she/he quenches her/his cigar on Bloom's ear; and riding
Bloom she/he squeezes his/her testicles (*U* 433–36). Bloom
ends up, in this fantasy, cheering on Boylan making love to
Molly:

> BOYLAN *(to Bloom, over his shoulder)* You can apply
> your eye to the keyhole and play with yourself while I
> just go through her a few times.
>
> BLOOM Thank you, sir. I will, sir. May I bring two
> men chums to witness the deed and take a snapshot? *(he
> holds out an ointment jar)* Vaseline, sir? Orangeflower
> . . . ? Lukewarm water . . . ? . . .
>
> BLOOM *(his eyes wildly dilated, clasps himself)* Show!
> Hide! Show! Plough her! More! Shoot! (*U* 462)

This may as well be a scene out of *Venus in Furs,* where
Wanda's infidelity is what most inflames Severin's passion.
"[P]ain holds a peculiar attraction for me [he explains] . . .
nothing kindles my passion quite so much as tyranny, cruelty
and above all unfaithfulness in a beautiful woman" (*VF* 149).
Wanda admits that she has admirers so as not to lose Severin—
to allure him all the more, to arouse his passion (*VF* 197).
Also like Richard Rowan in *Exiles* who sets himself up to
suffer over the possibility of Bertha's infidelity (and we will
get to Richard), Severin must endure Wanda's relationship
with the Blazes Boylan figure of *Venus in Furs:* Alexis Pa-
padopolis, "the Greek," a magnificent specimen of man, "A
man, in fact" (*VF* 208), possessing "fierce virility" (*VF* 210).
Masoch's account of his own pleasurably painful cuckoldry,
by Wanda, his wife, and Sandor, her lover, seems to provide
a real life model for the scene of happy torture in "Circe."
Describing his encounter with Wanda after he has witnessed,
through a keyhole, her lovemaking with Sandor, Masoch
writes in his diary: "We entered the room where Wanda had
surrendered to Sandor. . . . She threw off her corset and white

vest, resumed her white furs and lay down on the divan, her glorious bosom heaving slightly under the furs. 'Are you satisfied now?' she asked. I knelt at her feet. 'Oh, Wanda, you were so cruel to me!' I embraced and kissed her passionately. . . . '[Y]ou were splendid, truly cruel.' "[6]

That Bloom is a masochist and that Molly is his (primary) Venus in Furs leaks out even in the less fantastic portions of the book. Making his debut in *Ulysses,* Bloom meditates on the cruelty of his cat, finding it "curious" that "mice never squeal" but "seem to like it" (*U* 45). Bloom's cat cries "Mrkrgnao" (*U* 45); Molly utters "Mn" (*U* 46); and this feline parallel which makes Bloom a punishment-hungry mouse is nicely reinforced a few pages later: "Who's getting it up? [asks M'Coy]. Mrs Marion Bloom. Not up yet [thinks Bloom]. Queen was in her bedroom eating bread and. No book. Blackened court cards laid along her thigh by sevens. Dark lady and fair man. Letter. Cat furry black ball" (*U* 61). The letter from Boylan, Joyce's version of Masoch's "the Greek," juxtaposed with the cruel furry cat seems to identify Molly as a Venus in Furs. (Masoch himself, as one would expect, venerated cats. In the novel, Severin feels "like a mouse held captive by a beautiful cat who plays with it daintily, and at any moment is ready to tear it to pieces" [*VF* 169]; Wanda figures out that to Severin "a woman in furs is nothing more than a large cat, . . . a sort of highly charged electric battery" [*VF* 148].)

Inspired by Simon Dedalus's singing of *Martha* in "Sirens" to think about the cruelty of losing a loved one, Bloom decides, "Yet too much happy bores" (*U* 228). He clearly takes pleasure in Boylan's ability to "organise" his "Marion of the bountiful bosoms" (*U* 262). To Joe in "Cyclops," where for a while he withstands the antisemitism directed at him, Bloom compliments Boylan—"He's an excellent man to organise. Excellent" (*U* 262)—and Boylan obviously cooperates in playing his part in Bloom's drama of masochism. At center stage

Bloom seems as vulnerable to Molly's "whip" or to the power of the fetish as Joyce was (art imitates life and vice versa): he purchases black underclothes from Miriam Dandrade in the Shelbourne hotel (*U* 132), gives gifts of gloves to Molly (*U* 612), ejaculates after she stimulates him with her foot (*U* 614), and is generally fixated on drawers (Molly "promised to give him the pair off [her] doll to carry about in his waistcoat pocket" [*U* 614–15]).

Of course Molly and Bloom have help in figuring out proper masochistic etiquette: literature of masochism feeds them both. Educating her (as Deleuze says the masochist educates his Venus, and as Joyce educated Nora by giving her Masoch to read), Bloom brings home to Molly masochistic novels that he appears at least to skim: *Ruby: the Pride of the Ring* (one illustration of which shows a "fierce Italian with carriagewhip" [*U* 52]; this appears to be female not male masochism), *Tales of the Ghetto* by Leopold von Sacher-Masoch (which they had sometime in the past [*U* 193]), *Fair Tyrants* by James Lovebirch (which Bloom once got for Molly and she apparently disliked) (*U* 194), and *Sweets of Sin* (which reflects rather specifically the Molly/Boylan/Bloom masochistic *ménage à trois* paradigm [*U* 194]). Molly indicates that her adulterous act with Boylan is in effect a duplication of the plots of pulp novels such as these through her nocturnal mental wanderings: "because he [Bloom] has an idea about him [Boylan] and me hes [Bloom's] not such a fool he [Bloom] said Im dining out and going to the Gaiety" (*U* 610); "such an idea for him [Bloom] to send the girl [Milly] down there to learn to take photographs . . . on account of me and Boylan thats why he [Bloom] did it Im certain the way he [Bloom] plots and plans everything out" (*U* 630); and "Ill let him [Bloom] know if thats what he [Bloom] wanted . . . theres the mark of his [Boylan's] spunk on the clean sheet . . . that ought to satisfy him [Bloom]" (*U* 641). Her intuition that "it was . . . thinking about [her] and Boylan set him off" (*U* 611) is confirmed by

Bloom's "approximate erection" (*U* 604), the effect of his meditation on Molly's afternoon romp with Boylan. As if she thinks Bloom is not quite satiated, she entertains the fantasy of literally whipping him: "in his flannel trousers Id like to have tattered them down off him before all the people and give him what that one calls flagellate till he was black and blue do him all the good in the world" (*U* 629). Masochism is no secret subject of *Ulysses*.

Joyce fashions Nora into a Nora in Furs; Bloom fashions Molly into a Molly in Furs. But how does *Joyce* fashion Molly into a Molly in Furs who can offer him release from castration anxiety or, perhaps a better way to think of it, from the redoubtable punishing environment of his childhood? (*"Moly,"* Joyce wrote, "is a nut to crack. . . . Moly is the gift of Hermes, god of public ways, and is the invisible influence [prayer, chance, agility, *presence of mind,* power of recuperation] which saves in case of accident" [*SL* 272].) To return to Deleuze's stress on "formal elements of fictional art," how does Joyce's writing embody, enact, fulfill his masochistic drives? Again, these questions may for a while push us in a direction seemingly far afield from Catholic theology. But they lead to a psychopathology that entails a rebellion against Joyce's Catholic Fathers that gets worked out on the linguistic level of Joyce's text. The Masochian/Deleuzean masochistic model accounts for both the feminine and literary nature of that rebellion.

II

Venus in Furs receives her slave. I can see that you are far more than an ordinary romantic; you do not fall short of your dreams, you become the man you imagine yourself to be, though it means nothing less than folly. I must admit that I am impressed by your behaviour; it takes a certain strength, and one can only admire

*strength. I actually believe that in unusual circumstances
and in a more exalted age than this, what appears to be
your weakness would reveal itself as impressive power.*
—addressed to Severin by Wanda in *Venus in Furs*

To answer the question of how masochism is inscribed in
Joyce's writing, I first need to elaborate the specificities of
Joyce's masochistic aims. Since I have said that in the sub-
stitution of the whipping woman/"mother" for the whipping
fathers/Fathers Joyce was able to gain mastery he otherwise
would not have been able to achieve, it should be clear that
he was not solely out to get hurt or to sacrifice himself. For
this reason too the Deleuzean rather than Freudian model of
masochism needs to be invoked. For it is not that Joyce felt
he had transgressed against the father, as Freud proposes about
the masochist in general, or that he felt guilty over an Oedipal
crime, a parricidal urge, or original sin, as Shechner posits
about Joyce, and as a result felt compelled to undergo punishment.[7] Deleuze contests Freud's Oedipal interpretation of
masochism, replacing Freud's idea that "the masochist's aim
is to escape from the consequences of the transgression against
the father" (*M* 92–93)[8] with a maternal-oral etiology. Joyce
was too shameless and radically rebellious to worry about
such transgression and thus, like the Deleuzean masochist (he
was), took no interest in placating the father.

The Masochian/Deleuzean masochist "asks to be beaten,"
but, Deleuze asks, "Why and for what crime? Is it not precisely
the father-image in him that is thus miniaturized, beaten, ridiculed and humiliated? What the subject atones for is his resemblance to the father and the father's likeness in him: the
formula of masochism is the humiliated father. Hence the father is not so much the beater as the beaten" (*M* 53). Suffering
is "the necessary precondition" for achieving pleasure, which
can become available only once the father is ousted; the masochist has a plan. He is "insolent in his obsequiousness, re-

bellious in his submission; in short he is a humorist, a logician of consequences." The masochist—and this cannot be over-stressed in Joyce's case—"stands guilt on its head by making punishment into a condition that makes possible the forbidden pleasure" (*M* 78).

So the question can be reformulated more accurately: How does Joyce develop a literary strategy of masochism designed to retaliate against the flogging fathers/Fathers of Dublin and (perhaps more important) to beat their ghostly presence out of himself in an effort finally to achieve forbidden pleasure? We have traced already a great deal of the literary evolution of Joyce's masochism or, to put the idea synecdochically, Joyce's transformation of whip to reed. By the time he decided to reject the Catholic priesthood in favor of the priesthood of art, Joyce had taken the first step in a masochistic literary strategy. With the pen transmogrified in *A Portrait* from the sadistic fathers'/Fathers' stick, whip, pandybat, Joyce then re-produced literarily the theology of the Church. The Mysteries of the Eucharist, Incarnation, and Trinity as well as biblical hermeneutics appear variously in *Ulysses,* as we have seen at length. Joyce thereby establishes and displays his resemblance to the Father(s). But he subsequently translates biblical typology and these Mysteries into components of literature with such a vengeance that the very excessiveness of the reconstruction constitutes a main thrust of the dismantling. The insidious process empties out Catholic theology, allowing Joyce to empty—or beat—it out of himself. The very tedium, strictness, and cruel rigor of the project help show its masochism.

In a parallel move, as Catholicism fades, so do Joyce's representational words, the building blocks he uses to erect a literary simulacrum of Dublin—by no accident, the locus, the home, of his fathers/Fathers. Their preoccupation with virility, their sadism, their narrative/realism, all are subtly undermined but only again after Joyce reconstructs his resemblance to them. For at first Joyce marshals phallic artistic energy toward perhaps the most ambitious attempt ever to write a realistic novel. It is as if he, in the first half or so of *Ulysses,* believed he could "manfully" think up a signifier for every referent in Dublin; like Stephen, and in the spirit of the Aquinan realist, he would, fanatically, "recreate life out of life" (*P* 172). Although he had turned the whip into a reed, had become Thoth, and in a sense had distanced himself from Dublin insofar as his sheer ability to write about the dread city shows some detachment (not to mention that he displaced himself physically to continental Europe to write), what Joyce ended up reproducing initially was the world of repression his overall strategy was set up eventually to disavow—the representational style that predominates serving as an appropriate psychological equivalent (free play being anathema to realism) for the castrating fathers/Fathers he needed to expel from his literary universe.

In Joyce, as in Masochian/Deleuzean masochism, finally "the father is excluded and completely nullified" (*M* 53); "he is deprived of all symbolic function" (*M* 56). "[W]hat is beaten, humiliated and ridiculed in [the masochist] is the image and the likeness of the father, and the possibility of the father's aggressive return. *It is not a child but a father that is being beaten.* The masochist thus liberates himself in preparation for a rebirth in which the father will have no part" (*M* 58). The syndrome requires therefore that, just as Joyce invokes the Catholicism he means to undermine, he must humiliate himself in his initial phallogocentric drive. Explicitly from "Sirens" on (where the phallic is mocked) and implicitly from the start, Joyce punishes himself by sabotaging the representationalism of his *work* with the *text*uality of his play. He strains to father the world that fathered him, conscious that he is bound to fail, since signifiers produce a Text, not reality, since words on a page dance around, recombine capriciously, link up with unrelated words crazily, cancel out their referents anarchically. But Joyce relishes his play, delights in it precisely because it means the downfall of his own position as the ultimate phallic, Catholic realist. He was driven (literarily) to revive the fathers/Fathers provisionally to banish them permanently.

But, being a masochist, he needed a helpmate, a torturer (actually a "torturess") who could assist him in his liberation from his fatherly/Fatherly foes. In masochism, according to Deleuze, the victim invests "the totality of the law . . . upon the mother, who expels the father from the symbolic realm" (*M* 78). "The masochist experiences the symbolic order as an intermaternal order in which the mother represents the law under certain prescribed conditions; she generates the symbolism through which the masochist expresses himself" (*M* 55–56). The "torturess" becomes the new master—a complex triadic maternal figure. Deleuze locates in the writing of Masoch three fundamental mother images who in their unification expel the father from the masochistic universe: "the primitive, uterine hetaeric mother, mother of the cloaca and the swamps"; "the Oedipal mother, the image of the beloved, who becomes linked with the sadistic father as victim or as accomplice; and in between these two, the oral mother, mother of the steppe, who nurtures and brings death [to the old regime]" (*M* 49)—hence facilitating "a second birth, a parthenogenesis from which the ego re-emerges, liberated from the superego . . ." (*M* 112–13).

Joycean counterparts to the members of this matriarchal trinity may be located in *Ulysses*. Bella Cohen might be said to represent all the "hetaerae" in the book; in *Venus in Furs*, the masochist Severin is reading in *The Odyssey* about Circe, "the delightful witch who changed her suitors into wild beasts" (*VF* 131), when he first espies his Venus in the garden. May Dedalus certainly aligns herself with the sadistic Fathers in wishing to bind Stephen to the Church. And by virtue of her silent speaking, Molly fits Deleuze's description of the oral mother: "We call her intermediate [Deleuze writes], but she may also come last of all, for she is both oral and silent and therefore has the last word" (*M* 49). Joyce likewise gave the "last word" to Molly (*SL* 274). In the masochistic fantasy, the hetaeric and Oedipal mothers are eventually embodied in the oral mother: "The whole tendency of masochism is to idealize the functions of the bad mother and transfer them on to the good mother" (*M* 54). The extremes of "bad mother" behavior—promiscuity and sadism—are reconceived as "good" by the masochist because they are acted out under contract to him, for the sake of his sentimental but essentially aesthetic pleasure. According to the Hegelian dialectic enacted in Masoch, the sensuality of the hetaeric mother meets the repression of the sadistic mother to return as the severe sentimentality of the oral mother. Correlatively, Molly—a Mary figure antitypically fulfilling May Dedalus's role as a type of the Virgin—conflates Stephen's threatening mother with, given Molly's promiscuity, the hetaerae (the "Circean" prostitutes) of *Ulysses*. Molly fits the latter function rather snugly: "In Masoch . . . the ideal form of prostitution is based on a *private* contract whereby the masochist persuades his wife, in her capacity as good mother, to give herself to other men" (*M* 55).

In general Molly sounds a great deal like Deleuze's/Masoch's triumphant oral mother (triumphant in that she absorbs the two subsidiary, hetaeric and Oedipal mother-figures): Molly and Deleuze's/Masoch's oral mother are both earth-mother types. The masochist endows his mother-lover with an "amplitude" (*M* 59); "she is the common essence of agriculture, matriarchy and rebirth" (*M* 83). Molly imagines herself the next morning walking "over to the markets to see all the vegetables and cabbages and tomatoes and carrots and all kinds of splendid fruits all coming in lovely and fresh" (*U* 641). She would "love to have the whole place swimming in roses" (*U* 642)—but actually displays a varied floral taste, for primroses, violets, rhododendrons, jessamine, and geraniums. Supporting

Stuart Gilbert's sense of Molly as "Earth," Joyce wrote to Frank Budgen about her monologue: "It begins and ends with the female word *yes*. It turns like the huge earth ball slowly surely and evenly round and round spinning, its four cardinal points being the female breasts, arse, womb and cunt expressed by the words *because, bottom* (in all senses bottom button, bottom of the class, bottom of the sea, bottom of his heart), *woman, yes*" (*SL* 285). (Molly appears to be a mother/lover with a peculiarly linguistic constitution.) As for her matriarchal tendencies, even the first-time reader perceives that Molly at least seems to rule the roost at 7 Eccles Street. And in breathing new life, through her final memory, into Bloom's marriage proposal, she generates a feeling of rebirth at the novel's ("yes I said yes I will Yes") affirmative close.

But to observe how Joyce uses Molly as a cipher through whom he "speaks the language of the torturer he is to himself" (*M* 17), we must move beyond narrative. Despite the orality of Masoch's phallic mother, "it is essential to the masochist that he should . . . get her to 'sign' "; the masochist requires "contractual relations" with his torturess (*M* 20).[9] And to sign, Molly must naturally take possession of the pen, her appropriation of which plays an enormous role in her "whipping" of Joyce. We have followed the transformation of the whip to the pen. Now Joyce hands over the pen/penis/phallus to Penelope, who fantasizes about possessing the male organ— "I wished I was [a man] myself for a change just to try with that thing they have swelling up on you so hard" (*U* 638)— and who in turn employs that pen as a metaphorical whip to penalize Joyce. On the level of the narrative, Molly has a "fur" in the originary sense of that term for fetishists: speaking of Mrs. Riordan's dog, Molly complains, "and her dog smelling my fur" (*U* 608). To the extent that narrative disintegrates, becomes antinarrative, she wields the pen. Through her interior monologue, which seems both spoken mentally and written (perhaps it is best said that Molly speaks or reads her written contract with Joyce), Molly claims the most playful, serendipitous, nonlinear, nonrepresentational language of *Ulysses*. And thus, in retrospect, we may read all the earlier writing that served to subvert Joyce's phallic/Catholic/realist task as manifestations of her punishing strokes. (Though it might seem odd that play serves as punishment, this is precisely the setup the masochist seeks/needs to effect, turning pain into a condition that produces pleasure, and thus stamping out the fathers'/Fathers' law.) Upon observing Molly's claim on the language of play in *Ulysses* (Christine van Boheemen puts it this way: "The style of [Molly's] otherness is a figure for the otherness of the text as a whole"),[10] we can then understand the punitive aspect of Joyce's wordplay, a distinctive feature of it that we will see Joyce makes clear, as the "cruelty" of Molly Bloom.

Finding fault with Freud's position that the masochist lacks an ego, Deleuze shows that the masochist lacks, if anything, a superego, and that the ostensible weakness of his ego is "a strategy by which [he] manipulates the woman into the ideal state for the performance of the role he has assigned to her" (*M* 107). In Deleuzean masochism, the masochist's disavowal of the world of the father is "a process of liberation" that relieves him of "the pressures of the superego" and "that transfers to the oral mother the possession and privileges of the phallus" (*M* 109). This is in effect what Joyce does as he relinquishes the pen to his Penelope, so that she (like Homer's heroine) can weave a tapestry or, in other words, write a Text (despite the fact that textuality might normally undermine phallic power without simultaneously exercising it). "The plural of the Text [Barthes pronounces] depends . . . on what might be called the *stereographic plurality* of its weave of signifiers (etymologically, the text is a tissue, a woven fabric)."[11]

Like the unnamed "Venus in Furs" in *Giacomo Joyce*, Molly is a "lady of letters" (*GJ* 12) with "Cobweb handwriting" (*GJ* 1). Her leapfrogging from topic to topic—so rapidly that we tend to lose track of all the realistic details, while we concentrate on the undulating words—gives the impression of an arbitrary movement of signifiers. Unlike the stern fathers/Fathers of Dublin and the Church, Molly promotes play—"Let us have a bit of fun" (*U* 608)—and desire—"What else were we given all those desires for" (*U* 639). Unlike Joyce, she does not fret over getting facts straight. Her pronouns, especially "he," are often jumbled: a rather crucial concluding phrase, "and I thought well as well him as another," could as likely refer to Mulvey—an early boyfriend who merely kisses Molly in Gibraltar—as to Bloom proposing marriage (*U* 643–44). In a book that realistically marks each moment, her temporal sense is vague: "I never know the time even that watch he gave me never seems to go properly" (*U* 615). She is hazy about her age: "For the 4 years more I have of life up to 35 no Im what am I at all Ill be 33 in September will I what O well" (*U* 618). The murkiness of her world glues us to her words.

So does her wordplay. She puns: about Blazes Boylan, Molly thinks, "Tearing up the tickets and swearing blazes because he lost 20 quid" (*U* 617); describing an imagined picnic scene with Boylan in it, she envisions "little houses down at the bottom of the banks there on purpose but its as hot as blazes" (*U* 629). Amused by double entendres, she recounts her exchange in confession with Father Corrigan (and in the process decries the priest for both his prudishness and prurience): "He touched me father and what harm if he did where and I said on the canal bank like a fool but whereabouts on your person my child on the leg behind high up was it yes rather high up was it where you sit down yes" (*U* 610). She revolves the multiple meanings of surnames, including her own: "And the new woman bloomers . . . I suppose theyre called after him I never thought that would be my name Bloom when I used to write it in print to see how it looked on a visiting card . . . youre looking blooming Josie used to say after I married him well its better than Breen or Briggs does brig or those awful names with bottom in them Mrs Ramsbottom or some other kind of a bottom . . ." (*U* 626).

She jingles: "Jesusjack the child is a black" (*U* 611); "Silly women believe love is sighing I am dying" (*U* 624); "Wherever you be let your wind go free" (*U* 628); "Will you be my man will you carry my can" (*U* 630); "her vagina and her cochinchina" (*U* 633); and "O wasnt I the born fool to believe all his blather about home rule and the land league sending me that long strool of a song" (*U* 634). She has a facility for alliteration: "God spare his spit for fear hed die of the drouth" (*U* 618); "faded all that lovely frock fathers friend Mrs Stanhope sent me" (*U* 621); "no wonder that bee bit him better the seaside but Id never again in this life get into a boat with him" (*U* 629). She dismantles and transforms words: despite Bloom's early morning language lesson, Molly breaks down "metempsychosis" to "met something with hoses in it" (*U* 620). My point here is generalized in *The Novel as Family Romance:* the flow of the language of "Penelope," "transgressing the boundaries set by syntax and decorum," presents a "stylistic practice of the text . . . in a concentrated and heightened form. We might say that 'Penelope,' by repeating, clarifying, and intensifying . . . writing in the body of the text, affirms and signs the alterity of *Ulysses*" (*NFR* 173).

Perhaps most glaringly, Molly indulges in contradiction, thus further destabilizing the relation of signifier and signified; language is hardly a vehicle to truth for Molly. At one moment she is impressed with Boylan's "tremendous big red brute of a thing . . . like iron or some kind of a thick crowbar standing all the time he must have eaten oysters I think a few dozen . . . no I never in all my life felt anyone had one the size of that to make you feel full up . . ." (*U* 611). She cannot seem to get penises off her mind. She would like for variety to try a black man's (*U* 618); and she is drawn to the male member of the statue Bloom bought for her:

> I often felt I wanted to kiss him all over also his lovely
> young cock there so simple I wouldnt mind taking him in
> my mouth if nobody was looking as if it was asking you
> to suck it so clean and white he looks with his boyish face
> I would too in 1/2 a minute even if some of it went down
> what its only like gruel or the dew. [*U* 638]

Yet occasionally Molly seems to empower Joyce to criticize
the brutality of phallic power. Her sense of the animality of
Boylan and his overly masculine body is made vivid: "Like a
Stallion driving it up into you because thats all they want out
of you with that determined vicious look in his eye I had to
halfshut my eyes still he hasnt such a tremendous amount of
spunk in him" (*U* 611). She burlesques the male genitalia in
imagining "what a man looks like with his two bags full and
his other thing hanging down out of him or sticking up at
you like a hatrack no wonder they hide it with a cabbageleaf
. . . theyre always trying to show it to you . . . as if it was 1
of the 7 wonders of the world . . . I tried to draw a picture
of it before I tore it up like a sausage or something" (*U* 620).
Nonetheless, as we have seen, Molly wants a penis of her
own.

Perhaps it is no accident that her penchant for oscillation
manifests itself most strikingly on the subject of sexuality. The
evidence I use here thematizes the point that Molly makes no
final (masculine) claim to authority: she sometimes seems to
and then self-contradiction proves that she does not. Perhaps
she writes as a "woman" insofar as she at one moment praises
women and at another blames them, at one moment adores
male organs, at other times scorns them. That she wants a
penis and does not want one—or metaphorically has one and
does not have one—makes her the fetishized phallic mother
Joyce needed in order to do battle successfully with the authority he wished to overturn. It is not only that the fetishist
invests the mother with the phallus at the same time that he

feels at some buried level the anxiety that caused him to delude himself in the first place. But this point may be made most significantly at the level of language: Molly's oscillating style is antithetical to the rigid realism Joyce starts out with in *Ulysses,* and thus helps him to subvert it. Had her writing been merely a more powerful representational style, she would have been ineffective in driving out the paternalistic authority Joyce was reacting against. She would merely have rivaled and continued it. Through Molly and her strategically controlled playful prose, however, Joyce has a chance to move on to textual pleasure, after a bit of pain.

By presenting the chapter as a self-consciously written document, Joyce highlights the contractual aspect of "Penelope." Molly is Joyce's oral mother, but, again, she must also write since the same pen with which she signs the masochist's contract serves as her whip. Typography is unmistakable: numbers are printed as Arabic numerals ("hes about wait 88 I was married 88 Milly is 15 yesterday 89 what age was he then at Dillons 5 or 6 about 88" [*U* 637]). Molly's letter to Mrs. Stanhope appears as written: "with love yrs affly Hester x x x x x" (*U* 622). Even Molly's poor grammar and spelling identify the chapter as writing (no *spoken* difference exists between her errors that Joyce takes care to preserve and the correct forms they invoke by contrast). As if she were the novel's clever author punning self-reflexively, Molly refers to "books with a Molly in them" (*U* 622) (she dislikes *Moll Flanders*), to "general Ulysses Grant" (*U* 623), to Mulvey's ship, the "H M S Calypso" (*U* 626); and "there is a flower that bloometh" slips in out of nowhere (*U* 625). Reading over this material, Joyce might appropriately recall this half-sarcastic line from *Giacomo Joyce:* "My words in her mind: cold polished stones sinking through a quagmire" (*GJ* 13).

Perhaps especially all the structural underpinnings of the chapter—for instance, the repetition of the Mollyesque earthwords "because," "bottom," "woman," and "yes," and the eight "sentences" in conjunction with the eight negatives at the beginning of the eighth "sentence" (*U* 638), as well as with the eight "yeses" that complete the "sentence," the chapter, the book—prove best that, as MacCabe asserts, once we reach "Penelope," "we leave behind the world of representation" (MacCabe 124). "Penelope" ends the conflict between (also MacCabe's formulation) the "figure of the omnipotent father, who will fix an identity on his son" and "the text's deconstruction of the mechanisms of identification" (MacCabe 66).

For Joyce expiates the "crime" of his resemblance to his Dublin fathers/Fathers by, from the start of *Ulysses,* pitting his representational work (the writing of the phallogocentric realist) against his Mollyesque Text, Molly's chapter being the primary locus in *Ulysses* of what Alice Jardine has named "*gynesis*—the putting into discourse of 'woman' . . . the valorization of the feminine, woman, and her obligatory, that is, historical connotations, as somehow intrinsic to new and necessary modes of thinking, writing, speaking," the product of which is "a *gynema* . . . a reading effect, a woman-in-effect that is never stable and has no identity."[12] Before Joyce earns psychologically the right to "play," all linguistic play—all the gynetic language of his Text—is commensurate with "punishment."

Such literary masochism is effected as the aggressive textuality of the latter portion of the novel, beginning roughly with "Sirens," supersedes the excruciating mimesis of the former, ending roughly with "Wandering Rocks." Prior to "Sirens," in fact, before gynesis in *Ulysses* is in full swing, Joyce seems doubly self-flagellating. First, the sheer wealth of naturalistic detail involved in the reconstruction of Stephen's, Bloom's, and Dublin's lives betrays a tedium, a cruel rigor that Joyce put himself through; he shows a painstaking desire to overlook nothing. Second, each time he lets in self-conscious words and phrases (for example, "Listen: a fourworded wavespeech: seesoo, hrss, rsseeiss, ooos" [*U* 41]; "Who'll read the book? I, said the rook" [*U* 85]; "Besteglinton" [*U* 168]) as well as puns ("dogsbody" [*U* 5]; "gravely" in "Hades"; "The quaker librarian, quaking, tiptoed in, quake, his mask, quake, with haste, quake, quack" [*U* 171]), and other features of the Text/gynesis/the disruption of narrative (that is, the newspaper headlines of "Aeolus"; the list of characters of Buck's play, *Everyman His Own Wife;* the longer list of *Ulysses* characters greeting the viceregal cavalcade at the end of "Wandering Rocks"), Joyce defeats his own fanatically realistic purposes. What Joyce first constructs is exhausting, and, on top of that, he/she militates against it. As Joyce's literary Venus in Furs, Molly punishes Joyce in his capacity as the writer of realism obsessively out to reconstruct Dublin brick by brick. By dismantling his realism, she enables him to disavow the chastising material world he had felt compelled to build up meticulously. The artist looks on as Molly in Furs topples his neat pairings of signifiers and referents that kept Dublin intact.

That nonrepresentational language or the language of excess, which I have attributed to the playful pen of Molly (in Furs), has a punitive function is even dramatized literarily. In "Cyclops," the kinship of puns and punishment is conveyed in a punning description of flogging in the British navy ("rear-admirals" are part of the scene):

> —A rump and dozen, says the citizen, was what that old ruffian sir John Beresford called it but the modern God's Englishman calls it caning on the breech.
> And says John Wyse:
> —'Tis a custom more honoured in the breach than in the observance.
> Then he was telling us the master at arms comes along with a long cane and he draws out and he flogs the bloody backside off of the poor lad till he yells melia murder. [*U* 270]

It is no accident ("A man of genius makes no mistakes" [*U* 156]) that the first pun young Stephen mulls over in *A Portrait* is "belt" (*P* 9). "Belt" additionally may be read (on a third level) as an expression of the masochism inherent in an obsessed realist's paronomastic habit. (The multiple referents of a pun would rarely serve the reconstruction of a realistic scene, but instead explode into incongruous constituents of a Text.)

Puns and masochism converge again through Martha Clifford's playfully threatening lines to Bloom: "Please write me a long letter and tell me more. Remember if you do not I will punish you. So now you know what I will do to you, you naughty boy, if you do not wrote" (*U* 63–64). Punishment here becomes hard to avoid: Not to write, Martha warns (as Father Dolan warned), will lead to punishment, and to write, or at least to write a pun (which Bloom is apt to do), also leads to punishment since "pun" is short for "punishment," and "punishment" embodies "pun," and consequently turns into a self-reflexive one. Bloom picks up cannily on this point. Immediately upon perusing Martha's letter (which contains a yellow flower), he gives a virtuoso performance of floral punning on the subject of punishment: "Angry tulips with you darling manflower punish your cactus if you don't please poor forgetmenot how I long violets to dear roses when we soon anemone meet all naughty nightstalk wife Martha's perfume" (*U* 64). The language of flowers is cruel before it is pleasure-producing. In "Sirens," Bloom recalls, and rewrites, lines from Martha's epistle in a way that draws out the idea of punishment implicit in "pun": "The rum tum tum. How will you pun? You punish me? Crooked skirt swinging, whack by" (*U* 230). Joyce is exploiting the violence inherent in the pun, which is probably derived from "pangere," to prick or pierce; related words are "poniard," "pugilism," "pugnacious," "poignant," "punch," and "puncture."[13]

"Whipped" as he has been by Martha, Gerty, and Molly, Bloom uses in "Nausicaa" a stick, his "wooden pen" (*U* 312), to produce a masochistic conundrum: with fragments of Martha Clifford's ominous epistle invading his mind—"I called you naughty boy because I do not like"—Bloom inscribes "I. AM. A" in the sand (*U* 312). Though he effaces his words, the repetition (nine times) of *"Cuckoo"*—a pun on cuckold—at the chapter's end seems fittingly to complete his note to Gerty MacDowell (*U* 313). Bloom has been punished poignantly this June 16, 1904, and has the desire to pun on it.

Joyce's dramatization of the correlation in *Ulysses* of puns and punishment indicates the way that Molly's playful pen sabotages his realism; it points to her mode of facilitating Joyce not only in punishing himself for his lingering attachment to the fathers/Fathers but in carrying out his simultaneous onslaught on Church theology. That is, gynesis (a "woman-in-effect"), disrupted narrative, or linguistic excess is also exactly the extreme to which Joyce brings each of the Mysteries of the Church he secularizes as well as biblical hermeneutics. We have seen that (and how) Joyce slowly relegates biblical typology to the condition of wordplay through the extravagance of his secularization/textualization. He carries the motion from "Old Testament" to "New Testament" so far that not merely is a chain of typological signifiers set up, but signifiers take over. And we have watched his appropriation of the Eucharist, Incarnation, and Trinity shatter theology into textuality. I have argued that Joyce empties out all three Mysteries by situating their spiritual energy finally in linguistic play, so that this energy dissipates into the Text and so that the Name-of-the-Father is forced to join a relay of signifiers that precludes its supremacy and reveals its arbitrary, fraudulent status, fraudulent because it is merely legal, a legal fiction. (As Jane Gallop explains, "Lacan's Name-of-the-Father operates explicitly in the register of language. . . . [It] is the fact of the attribution of paternity by law, by language. Paternity cannot be perceived, proven, known with certainty; it must be instituted by judgement of the mother's word.")[14] *Ulysses* evolves from flesh/realism to word/self-conscious linguistic labyrinth, from Logos to logos, and from phallus to "womb of the imagination" (through its inversion of the Incarnation), and thus moves in the direction of "Penelope"/Molly—or we might say thereby manifests the activity of her punishing gynetic pen all along. And herein lies the brilliant ingenuity of the masochist: "The law now ordains what it was once intended to forbid; guilt absolves instead of leading to atonement, and punishment makes permissible what it was intended to chastise" (*M* 88)— that is, play. Joyce derisively, parodically, enforces the law of the fathers/Fathers—punishment—to void those fathers/Fathers and their law.

The masochist, in Deleuze's conception, postpones his pleasure, just as Joyce postpones the pleasure of his Text. Deleuze's masochist derives "preliminary pleasure from punishment," but the "real pleasure is obtained subsequently, in that which is made possible by the punishment" (*M* 77). By setting himself up to withstand Molly's punishment ("[his] words in her mind") after he has undergone degrading punishment from the fathers/Fathers, Joyce positions himself to experience the very pleasure that the fathers'/Fathers' law was intended to forbid. The fathers/Fathers flog in an effort to repress play and desire; Molly "flogs" Joyce in order to cancel in him any resemblance to his paternity, and consequently Joyce reaps the pleasure (what was unlawful) of "Molly's Text."

The female phallus, or in this case Molly's pen, serves as a protest of the ideal against the real, providing the masochist with a way of exorcising a painful awareness of reality. "The educational undertakings of Masoch's heroes, their submission to a woman, the torments they undergo, are so many steps in their climb towards the Ideal" (*M* 20). In submitting himself, through submitting his re-creation of Dublin and the Church, to Penelope's pen of pleasure, Joyce moves away from the real (the formidable world of Dublin) to the ideal ("the coldness of aesthetic suspense" [*M* 115])—to what turns out to be a phallic "womb of the imagination." The ideal is defined in Masoch as "a counterpart of the world" rather than a description of it, "capable of containing its violence and excesses" (*M* 33). In masochism the real world is disavowed and suspended, and the "suspense points to the new status of the ego and to the ideal of rebirth through the agency of the maternal phallus" (*M* 109–10). The mother's supremacy is eternal: Joyce gave the symbol of infinity to "Penelope." Christine van Boheemen's version of Joyce's eventual use of Molly resembles my own: "Closer reading of the text shows that the image of Molly Bloom is, indeed . . . mythic, because her character hinges on the ambivalent combination of contradictory qualities within the compass of one entity. If fairy tales are resolved and concluded by the timely and beneficent intervention of ambivalent 'characters' who mediate between opposites, *Ulysses* is resolved by the presentation of a woman with phallic qualities" (*NFR* 180–81).

In the masochistic fairy tale, then, the rebirth of the masochist entails a process of desexualization followed by resexualization. Desexualization liberates the masochist from the father's likeness; resexualization allows him to enjoy forbidden pleasures (*M* 113). The abolition of the father's likeness leads to the "birth of the new Man" (*M* 88). Like Bloom in "Circe," Joyce (in his writing) works through a masochistic process of becoming the "new womanly man" (*U* 403) and thus alleviates "castration anxiety." In masochism, finally, "femininity is posited as lacking in nothing and placed alongside a virility suspended in disavowal" (*M* 59). Contrary to MacCabe's argument, Joyce refuses to accept castration (rather he exhausts himself in developing an elaborate scheme to fight it) as he refuses to accept the loss of the fetish, but precisely through his fetishistic psychology whose victim is Molly (Joyce was a masochist, and, as Deleuze makes clear, fetishism "belongs essentially to masochism" [*M* 29]) arrives in a position linguistically to play.

We can now pick up on the question raised in chapter 1 of the feminist implications of the feminization of Joyce's pen. Joyce develops a style that only masquerades as *écriture féminine*. Stephen Heath is no doubt right in commenting that "for male modernist writers seeking an avant-garde dislocation of forms, a recasting of given identity into multiplicity, writing differently has seemed to be naturally definable as writing feminine, as moving across into a woman's place," an assertion Heath backs up with the example of Joyce, whose "two great novels [end] in 'female' monologue or polylogue, Molly Bloom, Anna Livia."[15] In *Gynesis,* Alice Jardine has shown extensively and impressively the male postmodernist writer's and theorist's compulsion to conceive of "the most radical moments of most contemporary disciplines [as] a new rhetorical space" called "Woman."

> "[S]he" may be found in Lacan's pronouncements on desire; Derrida's internal explorations of writing; Deleuze's work on becoming woman; Jean-François Lyotard's calls for a feminine analytic relation; Jean Baudrillard's work on seduction; Foucault's on madness; Goux's on the new femininity; Barthes's in general; Michel Serres's desire to become Penelope or Ariadne . . . "She" is created from the close explorations of semantic chains whose elements have changed textual as well as conceptual positions . . . from time to space, the same to other, paranoia to hysteria, city to labyrinth, mastery to nonmastery, truth to fiction.[16]

Through Joyce's desire to become Penelope (an urge thematized in Stephen's femininity and Leopold Paula Bloom's cross-dressing in "Circe"),[17] he may very well have made most of these shifts. But because Joyce comes to gynesis through masochism, an essentially fetishistic psychology, it seems naive, invalid, as well as somewhat of a mockery or perversion of feminism to propose, as MacCabe does (and he is by no means alone in this view), that *Ulysses* voices "female desire . . . that produces the space for an escape from neurosis" (MacCabe

129) and that "Penelope is simply the movement of the book all over again, the movement to writing and the speaking of female desire" (MacCabe 131) *without* accounting for MacCabe's own qualifications of these assertions: "if only in its masculine position" and "through a male pen." (With her preoccupation with the penis, Molly would make a curious writer of "female desire." Likewise, at the end of the book, it is Molly who inseminates Bloom with the bit of "seed-cake"—a symbol to Father Boyle of "both sperm and the fruit of the Garden of Eden.")[18] I have tried to account for that pen: rather than relinquish it to Molly, Joyce merely lends it to her so that she may help carry out his masochistic desire (not, as Freud would have it, to be beaten by, or to love, but) to exorcise his myriad fathers/Fathers.

Since MacCabe complains that "the neurotic refuses to accept that meanings, both sexual and linguistic, are constituted by difference, and, instead, demands constant identities uncontaminated by the world of absence and loss" (MacCabe 24), it is puzzling that he reads Molly Bloom, the voice of female desire, the neurotic's escape route, as "a body that will not be reduced to a lack" (MacCabe 132). For "lack," MacCabe stresses throughout his book, is what enables the production of desire: "It is only through the admission of lack, the acceptance of the signifier, that desire can function." MacCabe insists that "in a world of presence there is no absent object to be desired" (MacCabe 109–10). If Molly is not lacking, what would prompt her desire for completion?

In taking his argument more purely to the level of language, MacCabe contrasts narrative with discourse. "[N]arrative represses both the reality of language and of women" (MacCabe 50), whereas discourse "involves, at the linguistic level, a castration, a narcissistic wound which must be submitted to if one is to accede to the adult world" (MacCabe 95). Because Joyce, in MacCabe's view (and he is certainly right here), struggles against narrative through his presentation of an array of discourses, it seems (following MacCabe's logic) that Joyce "at the linguistic level" accepts castration, or in other words the presence/absence, desire/lack interplay within language, that constitutive interplay that narrative represses. Yet (perhaps because MacCabe worries about associating women with lack), when he gets to Molly, he produces a non sequitur: that Molly—"fatal to a fetishism predicated on a denial of female desire"—has "a body that will not be reduced to a lack" (MacCabe 132). What sort of desire, to reiterate, would/could that be, within MacCabe's Lacanian conception? In "The signification of the phallus," Lacan defines desire as split, exactly what fullness is not: as "neither the appetite for satisfaction, nor the demand for love, but the difference that results from the subtraction of the first from the second, the phenomenon of their splitting *(Spaltung)*."[19] Perhaps MacCabe is on his way at this moment in *James Joyce and the Revolution of the Word* to reconceive desire, beyond Lacan, as Cixous does in "The Laugh of the Medusa," or as Deleuze and Guattari do in *Anti-Oedipus,* as *unfounded* on lack/loss/absence. But, if so, he stops short.

There are two other possibilities, as I see it, both of which may be true. Possibly MacCabe expresses his own fetishistic impulse: throughout his study he insists on the instability of the subject, on the illusory nature of full presence, in particular the full presence that the representational work tries to exhibit (such a work refuses to acknowledge the absence "contaminating" it). One would think that to express (MacCabe's version of) female desire Molly would somehow have to accommodate lack, but MacCabe sees her as the plenitude he, at other moments of his book, decries as illusory. So MacCabe's own fetishism may be at work here, and/or perhaps he is responding theoretically to Joyce's. Molly *does* seem an object of plenitude; I have described her as possessing the "amplitude" required of the masochist's helpmate. While Joyce gives to her the language of play, language constituted by a play of differences, which one might expect would allow the speaking of desire (at least if one were to adopt Lacanian terms), fullness rather than loss comes across. Capturing the paradox, Christine van Boheemen writes: "There is a clear suggestion in the text that Molly is indeed to be taken as the embodiment of essential otherness, a new view of original presence, not metaphysical but physical, flesh rather than spirit, womb rather than phallus, flow rather than logos. . . . Joyce seems to be shifting the locus of origin from a phallocentric logos to a hypostasis of the idea of the 'other,' . . . thus invertedly continuing the practice of Western metaphysics" (*NFR* 178–79). Part of this effect has no doubt to do with the tight control that Joyce has over Molly's "play," which he uses to counter the father/Father—with his appropriation of it—so that the female voice goes unheard, is only ventriloquized. In fact, in his cooptation of "female desire," Joyce fits MacCabe's own description of the fetishist whose disavowal (of the woman's/mother's lack) allows *both* "a submission to an experience of language and the security of a dominant position" (MacCabe 126–27); Molly does not and does want/have a penis. It is too striking to ignore that MacCabe and/or Joyce disavows that Molly is lacking and the implications of that denial. They appear to claim the language of desire in "Penelope" as their own, making themselves the subject of desire and Molly the object, since her presumed fullness would keep her from being a desiring subject.

On a broader track, a wide spectrum of antipatriarchs exists; every rebellion against patriarchy is not an act of feminism, just as every linguistic disruption of realism and/or narrative is not a manifestation of "woman's writing." Joyce's language may occasionally seem, as Kristeva reads it, to " '[musicate] through letters,' resume within discourse the rhythms, intonations, and echolalias of the mother-infant symbiosis—intense, pre-Oedipal, predating the father,"[20] but to take this as an apt general description of Joyce's writing is to miss the aggressive (Aristotelian) realism of roughly the first half of *Ulysses* as well as Joyce's enormous investment in biblical hermeneutics and Catholic theology or in other words Joyce's need to undermine patriarchy not because of his otherness from it but precisely because of his resemblance to it. In Cixous's "The Laugh of the Medusa," mother's milk turns to the woman writer's "white ink"; in Joyce, the pen derives from whips, sticks, canes, and pandybats—different stories of literary genesis altogether.

III

And why are we interested in the soul of the writer? . . . [B]ecause of the insatiable modern preoccupation with psychology, the latest and most powerful legacy of the Christian tradition of introspection, opened up by Paul and Augustine, which equates the discovery of the self with the discovery of the suffering self. For the modern consciousness, the artist (replacing the saint) is the exemplary sufferer. And among artists, the writer, the man of words, is the person to whom we look to be able best to express his suffering. . . . The writer is the man who discovers the use of suffering in the economy of art—as the saints discovered the utility and necessity of suffering in the economy of salvation.

The cult of love in the West is an aspect of the cult of suffering—suffering as the supreme token of seriousness (the paradigm of the Cross). . . . [T]he sensibility we have inherited identifies spirituality and seriousness with turbulence, suffering, passion. For two thousand years, among Christians and Jews, it has been spiritually fashionable to be in pain. . . . The modern contribution to this Christian sensibility has been to discover the making

of works of art and the venture of sexual love as the two
most exquisite sources of suffering.
—Susan Sontag, "The Artist as Exemplary Sufferer," in
    Against Interpretation

A tighter connection can be made between Joyce's masochism
and his attachment (obviously tortured) to the Church. For
Joyce envisaged himself as a Christ figure not merely as token
of his messianism but also of his masochism: "The two principle [*sic*] male figures in Masoch's work are Cain and Christ"
(*M* 83). Of course Masoch's conception of Christ does not
exactly match that of the Church, though it does appear to
conform with the Christ-like role Joyce adopted. There is even
a certain Masochian ring to the names "Melancholy Jesus"
and especially "Crooked Jesus" that (as Ellmann mentions
[489]) Joyce gave to himself.

In Masoch's story "The Mother of God," the main character
Mardona (the Madonna figure) explains to her male "victim":
"It is the love of the Mother of God that brings redemption
and gives new birth to man." Consequently, "she asks that
he consent to be tortured, and orders him to be nailed to the
cross. . . . Mardona then enters into a painful ecstasy, while
at nightfall Sabadil [the masochist] enacts the Passion of
Christ. . . . The Mother of God must crucify her son in order
that he should truly become her son and enjoy the privilege
of a rebirth from her alone" (*M* 85). In a story about the life
of a seventeenth-century Messiah, Masoch's hero typically
undergoes torture (the oral mother-figure "crowns him with
thorns and whips him"), and upon inquiring, "Woman, what
have you done to me?" receives the reply, "I have made a
man of you" (*M* 86). This theme, which recurs in Masoch—
"You are not a man, I am making a man of you"—involves
the obliteration of the father and his likeness "to generate the
new man" (*M* 86). Genuine "Apostasy" lies in becoming a
man through the "woman alone, to undergo a second birth"

(*M* 86). Deleuze concludes: "The final objective of Masoch's work expresses itself in the myth that embraces both Cain and Christ: Christ is not the son of God, but the new Man" (*M* 87).

Generally speaking, in Masoch's version of the story of Christ,

> the likeness of the father is . . . abolished. ("Why hast thou forsaken me?"), but here it is the Mother who crucifies the Son; in the masochistic elaboration of the Marian phantasy, the Virgin in person puts Christ on the cross; this is Masoch's version of "the death of God". By putting him on the cross and thus placing him under the same sign as the son of Eve, the Virgin carries on the aim of the mother-goddess, the great oral mother: she ensures the partheno-genetic second birth of the son in his resurrection. But again, it is not the son who dies so much as God the Father, that is the likeness of the father in the son. The cross represents the maternal image of death, the mirror in which the narcissistic self of Christ (Cain) apprehends his ideal self (Christ resurrected). [*M* 84]

This is typology, but of a new sort: Cain and not Abel as prefiguration of Christ.

Joyce clearly had a Christ-like craving to be betrayed, one artistic expression of which we have already witnessed in Bloom. Joyce worked himself up to such a pitch over Nora's (harmless) dalliance with Vincent Cosgrave that he was compelled to ask her, "Is Georgie my son?" (*SL* 158). Especially his August 7, 1909, letter to Nora enacts a detailed drama of interrogation that positions her as his unfaithful tormentor. He asks, for example: "Did you place your hand on him as you did on me in the dark and did you say to him as you did to me 'What is it, dear?' " (*SL* 159). "I am tortured by memories," Joyce had written to Nora the previous day. Cosgrave's claim that he had made love to Nora turned out to be false, but while it lasted certainly provided Joyce with fruitful raw material that he could twist into cause to feel abused by her. That he wanted to be in a state of jealous doubt over Nora's sexual overtures to other men becomes plain. He took pleasure in noticing her attraction for other men: "With old friends Joyce sometimes boasted of the interest of other men in his wife, as he would make Bloom do later" (Ellmann 315–16). He encouraged a journalist named Prezioso to visit Nora, only to explode into anger once Prezioso "endeavored to become Nora's lover" (Ellmann 316). Ellmann rightly acknowledges the "self-laceration" involved in the Prezioso incident, but at the same time a reward was in the making, since Joyce was living out/creating the plot of *Exiles*. Later in their lives, Nora literally played the stage role of Bertha in *Exiles* and suffered as a result of the ambiguity of her character's behavior—which Joyce wished her to adopt.

> She was in tears one day because, as she confided to Frank Budgen, "Jim wants me to go with other men so that he will have something to write about." She seemed to have failed him in this wifely duty. She indulged him, however, to the extent of writing a letter to him in Locarno with the salutation, "Dear Cuckold," which indicates that it had become a marital game to tease him about a subject once inexpressibly tender. [Ellmann 445]

This is all to say that Joyce took pleasure in self-directed pain; but I do not want to lose track of the point that he did so, in his own conception, as a Masochian Christ. To Stanislaus (in 1905) he wrote: "Give me for Christ' sake a pen and an ink-bottle and some peace of mind and then, by the crucified Jaysus, if I don't sharpen that little pen and dip it into fermented ink and write tiny little sentences about the people who betrayed me send me to hell. After all, there are many ways of betraying people. It wasn't only the Galilean suffered that" (*SL* 76)—an outburst that not only establishes a parallel between Joyce and Christ but specifies writing as a means of revenge for the betrayal he felt he suffered. But perhaps Richard Rowan in *Exiles* best focuses the Christliness of Joyce's Masochian/Deleuzean masochism. In "Notes By the Author," Joyce aligns Richard with Christ through his description of Bertha—"Her tears are of worship, Magdalen seeing the rearisen Lord in the garden where he had been laid in the tomb" (*Exiles* 118)—and states outright that "Richard's Masochism needs no example." Joyce is not speaking loosely here. He has Masoch firmly in mind: he characterizes the play as "a rough and tumble between the Marquis de Sade and Freiherr v. Sacher Masoch" (*Exiles* 124).

Insofar as Richard sets himself up to be persecuted by Bertha's possible infidelity to him with Robert (just as Joyce positioned Nora to torment him), *Exiles* is about Masochian/Deleuzean masochism. Robert pledges his faith to Richard in a way that implicitly invokes Christ: "I will fight for you still because I have faith in you, the faith of a disciple in his master." And Richard (conforming with Masoch since the Masochian masochist must have a betrayer he can manipulate) reminds Robert that "there is a faith still stranger than the faith of the disciple in his master," and that is "the faith of a master in the disciple who will betray him" (*Exiles* 44). Richard, the "betrayed," contrives the possibility of the act of betrayal; like his exile, Richard's sexual suffering is willed. He admits this to Robert: "In the very core of my ignoble heart I longed to be betrayed by you and by her—in the dark, in the night—secretly, meanly, craftily. By you, my best friend, and by her. I longed for that passionately and ignobly . . ." (*Exiles* 70).

In typical Masochian masochistic fashion, there was to be a payoff in the end. Richard's purpose is "to build up [his] soul again out of the ruins of its shame" (*Exiles* 70). Bertha's name unveils paronomastically Richard's masochistic aim (for which she is indispensable), nicely conflating instrument (Bertha) and goal (rebirth). She is both cognizant of, and willing to articulate, her role in the scheme: "I am simply a tool for you" (*Exiles* 74). After all, she has lent psychological strength to Richard in the past: echoing the Masochian heroine's/oral mother's words, she confides tellingly to Beatrice, "I made him a man" (*Exiles* 100). (This is also how Joyce described Nora's transformation of him: "I am speaking now to the girl I loved, who had red-brown hair and sauntered over to me and took me so easily into her arms and made me a man" [*SL* 159].)

To complete her job in making Richard "a man," Bertha must become "the cruel mother," to borrow her words, that she claims is the image Richard is trying to get Archie to perceive her as (*Exiles* 52). She must act within Richard's masochistic theater in a way that leaves him with "a deep, deep wound of doubt in [his] soul" (*Exiles* 112), which is, to state the obvious, what happens. But, rather than being destabilizing or merely painful without recompense, the infliction of this wound—because it is inflicted by the mother and thus signifies her power—is finally enabling. What it enables Richard to do is to write. During the evening in which Bertha and Robert are together *possibly* consummating their relationship, Richard is, it seems furiously, setting pen to paper. "I wrote all the night," he announces to Robert (*Exiles* 109). We recall that, according to Bertha, Richard got "excited" when she confessed to him the particulars of her kissing session with Robert (*Exiles* 81). Richard tried to pry all the juicy information out of her, painful detail by painful detail. That excitement over the possible affair gets channeled into a desire to write. Masoch himself wrote quantitatively and qualitatively better after a whipping spree.

That Richard uses Bertha to help him achieve some sort of liberation would probably be disputed by no one. Joyce in his "Notes By the Author" corroborates such a description of the play's central struggle; it is in fact as if a "female principle" (not just one woman) is required. Richard is "fighting for his own hand, for his own emotional dignity and liberation in which Bertha, no less and no more than Beatrice or any other woman is coinvolved." Joyce gets more specific than this about Bertha's, or the woman's, role in a way that again evokes the parallel between Richard and Christ and that reinforces the play's debt to Masoch:

> [Richard] does not use the language of adoration and his character must seem a little unloving. But it is a fact that for nearly two thousand years the women of Christendom have prayed to and kissed the naked image of one who had neither wife nor mistress nor sister and would scarcely have been associated with his mother had it not been that the Italian church discovered, with its infallible practical instinct, the rich possibilities of the figure of the Madonna. [*Exiles* 120–21]

In the spirit of Masoch's Christ, Richard does not worship the Madonna or any woman but makes use of Bertha as the Madonna, as if the alleged Mariolatry of the Catholic Church were intended for the purposes of a masochist's delight.

Molly Bloom's performance in Joyce's masochistic drama can be translated into these same "religious" terms, her identification with the Mother of God being (at this point in Joyce criticism) well documented to the point of cliché. But I want to present instances of fusion nonetheless to show that—as well as how—Joyce implicates the Virgin in the production of the pleasure of the Text: Mary is positioned in "Penelope" on the border between identity and its dissolution.

In Masoch's *Venus in Furs*, a young German painter paints Wanda as "a Madonna, a Madonna with red hair and green eyes!" (*VF* 202). In a sense, in painting Molly's portrait, Joyce subtly follows his lead, though Molly becomes an analogue of the Virgin metonymically. Skewed trivial association gradually effects an identification. Earlier in the night, before Molly's monologue, thunder woke her so that she "thought the heavens were coming down about us to punish us ... like those awful thunderbolts in Gibraltar as if the world was coming to an end," and so she blessed herself and "said a Hail Mary" (*U* 611). She recollects having sung "Ave Maria" on the evening Bartell dArcy kissed her (*U* 614); and "in fine voice" she has performed "the *Stabat Mater* of Rossini" (*U* 67). She thinks of a statue of "the infant Jesus in the crib at Inchicore in the Blessed Virgins arms" (*U* 619). And in remembering displeasing Mrs. Rubio by not attending "mass often enough in Santa Maria," Molly recalls mockingly "all her [Mrs. Rubio's] miracles of the saints and her black blessed virgin with the silver dress" (*U* 625). Just after conjuring up Mrs. Rubio's "black virgin," Molly recollects "singing ... shall I wear a white rose" (*U* 625).

The most prevalent women's names in the chapter invoke Dante's white rose: Molly complains about her former servant Mary Driscoll (*U* 609); she dredges up the cornerboys' bawdy song about "my aunt Mary has a thing hairy" (*U* 638–39) and recounts a mishap over soup when she and Bloom went to the "Mallow Concert at Maryborough" (*U* 616); reflecting on Simon Dedalus, Molly remembers that "he was married at the time to May Goulding" (*U* 637); and she ponders Mrs. Maybrick's poisoning her husband (*U* 613). Molly curses by invoking the names Mary and May: criticizing Bloom's drawers fetish, she thinks to herself, "O Maria Santisima" (*U* 615); envisioning Denis Breen and the "postcard U p up" that has aggravated his craziness, she thinks to herself "O sweetheart May" (*U* 613). And the month Molly remembers and imagines most frequently is May. Pressing Boylan's hand she sings, "The young May moon shes beaming love" (*U* 609); she lights a candle in Whitefriars street chapel (after saying her "Hail Mary") "for the month of May" (*U* 611); and her rendezvous in nature with Mulvey takes place in "May yes it was May when the infant king of Spain was born" (*U* 625). The names

"Molly" and "May" themselves roughly conflate Virgin and Venus: the O.E.D. definition of "Molly" reads, "A familiar pet-form of the name *Mary;* often applied contemptuously to a 'lass', 'wench,' and occas. to a prostitute"; "May" is defined on the one hand as "A maiden, virgin," and on the other some ancient writers connected the Latin name for the fifth month of the year with the name of *Maia,* the goddess of fertility.[21]

Unveiling the Virgin's more covert complicity in the linguistic labyrinth of *Ulysses,* and thus her role as Molly's co-conspirator in disrupting linear narrative, allusions to the Virgin are interwoven into "Penelope" in an even finer, less representational way. The Virgin is not only conflated with Venus, but with the spirit of textuality. The number eight becomes her sign: the Immaculate Conception is December 8, and the Nativity of the Virgin September 8. Molly too has a claim on this number, her birthday being September 8. She remembers that, early in Bloom's courtship of her, he sent her "the 8 big poppies because [hers] was the 8th" (*U* 615). Hence the number becomes a twin reference to Mary and her earthly avatar, a kind of code. And there is no scarcity of eights in the chapter to which to apply it. Molly comments that she and Bloom have been married "16 years" (*U* 635)—two eights—and that they were married in "88" (a number she repeats—"88 I was married 88") (*U* 637). Eight "sentences" comprise the chapter; eight negatives lurk in the first sixteen words of "sentence" eight—"no thats no way for him has he no manners nor no refinement nor no nothing" (*U* 638);[22] and eight yeses end symmetrically the eighth "sentence." Trivial reinforcements of the importance of the number eight surface in Molly's report that Floey Dillon "wrote to say she was married to a very rich architect . . . with a villa and eight rooms" (*U* 624), as well as in the outcome of Molly's cards that morning, part of which is "the 8 of diamonds for a rise in society . . . and 2 red 8s for new garments" (*U* 637). Molly's breasts, not to mention her bottom, reiterate the eight configuration. In all these ways, "Penelope" is Mary's chapter, but Mary is Eve is Molly is Venus is femininity is textuality: Catholicism through Mary blesses Joyce's textual rebellion.

It is probably sheer coincidence that the number that becomes a sign of the Virgin, and Molly, when turned on its side suggests female breasts—the fetishization of which Joyce himself was preoccupied with. But whether or not the number eight is read fetishistically, Joyce's invocation of the Virgin raises the subject of fetishism in more than one way. It might, first of all, appear that the extravagance of Joyce's alignment of the Virgin Mary and Molly, the glaring gaps between the Virgin and what turns out to emblematize her—an eight, for example—simply continues Joyce's subversion of the Fathers through parody and the language of play. As in Joyce's textualizing of biblical hermeneutics, the Eucharist, Incarnation, and Trinity, here words and numbers—hollowed rather than hallowed signs—take over eventually at the expense of any holiness attached to the Virgin. And this diminution is certainly operating. In fact, to the extent that Joyce's fetishizing (in the sense of preserving the life of the sign over that of the referent) empties out the Virgin's conventional theological significance, it allows Joyce in a Masochian move to appropriate the Virgin as his—rather than the Fathers'—ally. That is, insofar as Joyce strips the Virgin of her religious robes, he maintains his assault on the Fathers; yet she is not the object of assault but is revealed to be a helpmate in it. The process splits her into her Virginal self faithful to the Fathers—in which capacity she is divested of theological value—and into her powerful maternal self useful to the son. Thus Joyce, as apostate Catholic, capitalizes on the related Protestant charges against Catholicism—Mariolatry and fetishism—as if to find within Catholicism, taken at its worst, taken as if Catholicism itself were apostasy, the means for his rebellion.

Joyce's act of appropriating the Virgin consequently entails fetishization in another sense, in a psychoanalytic sense. Joyce casts the Virgin in the role of a Masochian Madonna-figure who first punishes him: the Virgin, like Molly, is identified with disruptive language that helps crush Joyce's own masterful literary/theological urges inherited from the fathers/Fathers. And she thereby saves him: she is presented as being complicit in the production of a playful style of writing that finally gives him pleasure. The built-in phallic nature of the Virgin helps make the point of psychoanalytic fetishization: it is no accident (in more ways than one) that Joyce aligns his Venus with the immaculate Mother of God who is sufficiently potent to generate a Son without being deflowered. Especially in *A Portrait,* in which Stephen relies over and over again on the Virgin Mary to help him recover from injury from the Fathers, it is clear that for Joyce she was the most soothing, nonthreatening figure of the Church, the phallic-mother being, as we know, just what the masochist requires, despite the threat she might pose for others. Fresh from sinning with the prostitute, Stephen is not humiliated before her; he is instead uplifted by her.

> The glories of Mary held his soul captive: spikenard and myrrh and frankincense, symbolising the preciousness of God's gifts to her soul, rich garments, symbolising her royal lineage, her emblems, the lateflowering plant and lateblossoming tree, symbolising the agelong gradual growth of her cultus among men. . . . His sin, which had covered him from the sight of God, had led him nearer to the refuge of sinners. . . . If ever he was impelled to cast sin from him and to repent the impulse that moved him was the wish to be her knight. [*P* 104–05]

Even here, in speculating about being the Virgin's knight, Stephen's inclination is to make her power into his. Stephen/Joyce too has discovered "the rich possibilities of the figure of the Madonna."

In a skewed way (if I may digress from Molly for a moment, only to return immediately to Mary), so has Bloom in Gerty MacDowell: the psychology as well as its theological correlative is pervasive. The glaring parallel in "Nausicaa" between the Virgin Mary and Gerty—given Gerty's status as a fetishized female, given her role as Gerty in Furs—underlines the Virgin's fetishized identity. Mary is depicted as "most merciful," even as she is "most powerful" (*U* 291): "The reverend father Father Hughes had told them what the great saint Bernard said in his famous prayer of Mary, the most pious Virgin's intercessory power that it was not recorded in any age that those who implored her powerful protection were ever abandoned by her" (*U* 292). (Like *Moly,* the Virgin saves in case of accident.) Like Gerty, the Virgin attends to "wounds that wanted healing with heartbalm" (*U* 293). She keeps men from being lost: "Refuge of sinners. Comfortress of the afflicted. *Ora pro nobis.* . . . whosoever prays to her with faith and constancy can never be lost or cast away" (*U* 294).

This "mystical rose" (*U* 295) emerges as Molly's cohort in a Venus/Virgin scheme to punish and thereby save Joyce. She might be regarded as even more complicitous in the gynesis of the Text than Molly since rather than taking shape as a bona-fide character, the Virgin is constituted in "Penelope" solely through the play of language, through allusions and metonymic signals, such as the color white, the names Mary and May, the number eight. What is even more striking is that if the Virgin's, like Molly's, means of liberating Joyce from the Fathers is (metaphorically speaking) a pen that produces linguistic excesses—since such excesses are in *Ulysses* the means by which the Fathers' theology is reduced to wordplay and thus toppled—there would seem to be a link between Joyce's fetishizing (emptying out, overdoing) Catholic theology and his fetishizing (in the psychoanalytic sense) of Molly and the Virgin Mary. That is, the process by which Joyce evacuates Church theology of its meaning—since it is the very ploy of the fetishized mother/Madonna-figure lending him a hand in his struggle against the Fathers—is perhaps more than it at first seems. That Joyce aligns the very textuality to which he brings Catholic theology with Molly and Mary, that in other words he marks the move from theology to linguistic excess with the sign of woman/the Sirens/Molly/Penelope/Mary, would help to make the point.

Father Boyle, in his essay on "Penelope" in the Hart and Hayman collection, gives us a further clue: "Molly Bloom, like Cleopatra and like the Wife of Bath and like Hester Prynne, is not determined to univocal meaning."[23] We have already focused on Hester Prynne's embroidery and recognized its kinship with Catholicism. If Hester's linguistic finery bears affiliation with the Catholic Church, it seems plausible that so would Molly's, especially since Molly weaves in a largely Catholic, however apostate, linguistic universe. I have argued that Joyce deploys strategies of language to subvert the law of the Fathers; and I am certainly not retracting that thesis. This is not to say, however, that the strategy he deploys is absolutely alien to the object it is meant to undermine. All along I have argued the opposite—that Joyce's modes of rebellion against the Church always grow up out of Church soil. And so it seems perfectly appropriate that Joyce's use of linguistic excess/gynesis, though it sabotages Church patriarchy, keeps very much alive—if not helps to restore or reconstruct—the Church, only as a feminine body, with the Virgin as its head. Perhaps it would have been a different story if the Virgin Mary were not hiding in the linguistic interstices of Joyce's coda, or (what has even more weight) if Joyce had not brought Catholic theology to textuality and Molly/Mary simultaneously. We have seen, for example, that the slide in *Ulysses* from Christ's to Molly's blood sets in motion a network of linguistic play (primarily puns on flowers); it is partly insofar as Molly is paronomastically a "flower" (is menstruating) that she replaces Christ as host. Joyce's Incarna-

tional wordplay results in a proliferation of puns, especially
on the Virgin. And his parturition of the Word—a feminine
birth-giving in the "womb of the imagination"—identifies his
text/*textus*/tapestry as a piece of embroidery woven by a
woman; the Trinitarian artistic paradigm gives way to that
of the Virgin birth.

Hence verbal play—an antipatriarchal device—turns out to
be equivalent, in psychological terms, to the phallic force of
the mother/Madonna-figure since it is the result of Joyce's
giving her a pen to use playfully, antirepresentationally (but)
on his behalf—to promote his liberation. (Joyce is always in
command. He mocked the nonchalant attitude of his friend
McAlmon, who, in helping him with "Penelope," felt apathetic
about mixing up some of Molly's thoughts, since naive
McAlmon felt "it didn't much matter in what order her un-
systematic mind took them up" [Ellmann 514].) Joyce's ludic
writing testifies to Derrida's suggestion in *Spurs* that to have
style—synonym of "woman"—is to avoid being castrated in
that it is to pull oneself out of the castration/truth dynamic.
Derrida writes that "feminine distance abstracts truth from
itself in a *suspension* of the relation with castration."[24] But
this "protection against the terrifying, blinding, mortal threat
(of that) which *presents* itself, which obstinately thrusts itself
into view"[25] (a protection that sounds very much like a function of, rather than suspension beyond, castration anxiety)
comes at a price, at the expense of women. (Spivak has a
similar caveat about Derrida himself, questioning whether his
critique can "provide us a network of concept-metaphors that
does not appropriate or displace the figure of woman."
Though she realizes that it was inevitable that "woman's style"
become exemplary for the deconstructive philosopher, since
"*his* style remains obliged to depend upon the stylus or stiletto
of the phallus," Spivak explains why women must remain
wary of such glorification. Though deconstruction "is illu-
minating as a critique of phallocentrism," "as a 'feminist'

practice itself, it is caught on the other side of sexual difference.")[26]

Style in Joyce, *insofar as* it has the capacity to protect, serves
fetishistically as a counter-phallus. "Woman's style" is thus
paradoxically attractive: Joyce may wish to practice it because
of its aloofness from the castration/truth dynamic, but insofar
as he appropriates it to protect him, it becomes resituated
within this psychological dualism. For such a crutch, Joyce
appropriately invokes the Virgin to assist him in spinning out
an elaborate linguistic network where style reigns. (Discerning
the Mariolatry in Joyce's gesture toward women and "wom-
en's style," Christine van Boheemen writes that "his Mariolatry, his identification with the language of the 'other,' should
not be understood as acceptance of the feminine as 'other'
and willingness to open up to the castrating threat of materialism. Joyce's experimentation with language and logos is
not a tribute to a real womanhood of flesh and blood but has
from its inception been rooted in the supremacy of the imagination over matter, language or text over physical presence"
[*NFR* 191].) This is Joyce's sophisticated literary equivalent
of Farrington's son's desperate cry. Its roots go back, in other
words, all the way. The boy utters in "Counterparts" a "squeal
of pain as the stick cut his thigh"; he forms his hands in an
attitude of prayer to solicit help in his doomed struggle against
his already doomed father:

> —O, pa! he cried. Don't beat me, pa! And I'll . . . I'll say
> a *Hail Mary* for you. . . . I'll say a *Hail Mary* for you, pa,
> if you don't beat me. . . . I'll say a *Hail Mary*. . . . [*D* 98]

On the Masochian plan, then, Joyce looks to the Mother of
God, whom he manipulates into position, to protect and free
him—Son-of-God or rather "new Man" or "new womanly
man"—from the fathers/Fathers. Such dependency and ma-
nipulation are enacted, on the level of language, as Joyce spins
out—through the agency of the Virgin—linguistic embroidery

for the sake of overthrowing the fathers'/Fathers' theology/ realism/narrative. (Perhaps this is why "the artist, like the God of the creation, remains within or behind or beyond or above his handiwork, invisible, refined out of existence, indifferent, paring his fingernails" [*P* 215], because he is a concealed "she" who embroiders and has feminine habits.) By the end of *Ulysses*, the Fathers, and their law, may very well be abolished. But in a sense the Church—as a feminine (albeit phallic) body, led by Mother Mary, in whom Joyce has invested all his strength—prevails. Always attracted to the excessive (feminine) detail intrinsic to the Catholic aesthetic, Joyce spoke out against Wyndham Lewis's objection to "the cathedral at Rouen because of its heavily encumbered facade, which [Lewis] described as 'a fussy multiplication of accents, demonstrating a belief in the virtue of *quantity.*'" Joyce countered with his appreciation of "this multiplication of detail and added, 'As a matter of fact, I do something of that sort in words'" (Ellmann 515).

Although Joyce begins heavily parturiating words as if he were God-the-Father generating His Son, he ends as if inhabiting a female body (or at least in female dress) that enables him to dance on the border between representation and free play, a realm of light beyond communication. Kristeva writes that this border may be reached "only by virtue of a particular, discursive practice called 'art.'" Or, if one is a woman: it may be attained "through the strange form of split symbolization (threshold of language and instinctual drive, of the 'symbolic' and the 'semiotic') of which the act of giving birth consists" (*DL* 240). In a sense Joyce (being an artist and writing "as a woman" giving birth) tried to collate these activities, finally in "Penelope" using the Virgin Mary to guide him to the edge dividing symbolic coherence from a nonsymbolic, nonpaternal linguistic space of rhythm, light, poetry, eroticism, bliss— without allowing him to fall over the precipice.

The Virgin has always been located at just this verge; as Kristeva writes, "through the maternal body (in a state of virginity and 'dormition' before Assumption), [Christian reason] establishes a sort of subject at the point where the subject and its speech split apart, fragment, and vanish" (*DL* 237). Recognizing that "Christianity is doubtless the most refined symbolic construct in which femininity . . . is focused on *Maternality*," Kristeva defines *"maternality"* as the "ambivalent principle that is bound to the species, on the one hand, and on the other stems from an identity catastrophe that causes the Name to topple over into the unnameable that one imagines as femininity, non-language or body."[27] (It is ironic that "the orthodox constituent of Christianity, through John Chrysostom's golden mouth, among others, . . . sanctioned the transitional function of the Maternal by calling the Virgin a 'bond', a 'middle' or an 'interval.' ")[28] On the one hand, the Virgin grants access to what precedes identity; on the other, she serves as (Joyce's manipulated) "master" of this space, so that he can hold his own against the fathers/Fathers. Thus (like a Masochian torturess) she honors what Kristeva calls "the social–symbolic–linguistic contract." Joyce shifts the law over to the mother from the fathers/Fathers so that she can assist him in a finely tuned, precisely controlled subversion, not so that he can lose himself.

And not so that *her* desire rather than his may be expressed. It is not her but his pleasure that is at stake, a bliss or revery he can enjoy because she is helping him to be in control; Joyce is a fetishist, not a feminist. Kristeva's reading of Bellini's use of the Virgin seems descriptive also of Joyce's: "A kind of incest is . . . committed, a kind of possession of the mother, which provides motherhood, that mute border, with a language; although in doing so, he deprives it of any right to a real existence (there is nothing 'feminist' in Bellini's action), he does accord it a symbolic status. . . . [T]he result of this attitude . . . is a fetishized image, but one floating over a luminous background, evoking an 'inner experience' rather than a referential 'object' " (*DL* 249). It is the fetishized image of the Mother/Virgin that assists Joyce in getting beyond the referential, beyond the Father. But the reality of women remains ignored; fetishistic disavowal allows textuality or free play even as it provides the security of a dominant position—only the son's (disguised as the mother's) rather than the father's. As if expressing the Masochian supplanting of the Father by the Mother/Virgin, Bellini's *The Sacred Allegory* situates Mary on the throne: she assumes "the place of the Father" (*DL* 269). Like Bellini, Joyce needed to substitute for the law of the Father that of the Mother/Virgin in order to achieve his own artistic freedom.

Notes

Chapter 1. From Whip to Reed

1 This is the version in *Selected Letters* (14). In the final published form in *Chamber Music* (where the poem appears last), the concluding line is "My love, my love, why have you left me alone?"

2 Mark Shechner, *Joyce in Nighttown: A Psychoanalytic Inquiry into Ulysses* (Berkeley: Univ. of California Press, 1974) 36.

3 Joyce wrote in a letter to Grant Richards that was part of the negotiations over printing *Dubliners:* "The printer denounces *Two Gallants* and *Counterparts*. A Dubliner would denounce *Ivy Day in the Committee-Room*. The more subtle inquisitor will denounce *An Encounter*, the enormity of which the printer cannot see because he is . . . a plain blunt man" (*SL* 83).

4 Morris Beja not only traces this line of victimizers and victims, but he extends it to the epiphanies, *Stephen Hero,* and *Finnegans Wake*. See "The Wooden Sword: Threatener and Threatened in the World of James Joyce," *James Joyce Quarterly*, 2 (Fall 1964):33–41.

5 I quote here Mark Shechner (147), who is paraphrasing Theodore Reik, *Masochism in Modern Man* (New York: Farrar and Straus, 1941).

6 Jane Gallop, *The Daughter's Seduction: Feminism and Psychoanalysis* (Ithaca: Cornell Univ. Press, 1982) 63, 65.

7 Mary Colum and Padraic Colum, *Our Friend James Joyce* (Garden City, New York: Doubleday, 1958) 207.

8 Jacques Derrida, *Spurs: Nietzsche's Styles,* trans. Barbara Harlow (Chicago: Univ. of Chicago Press, 1978) 93.

9 Jacques Lacan, *Le Séminaire livre xx: Encore* (Éditions du Seuil, 1975) 56, quoted in (and translated by) Gallop 55.

10 Colin MacCabe, *James Joyce and the Revolution of the Word* (London: MacMillan Press, 1978) 63, hereafter cited parenthetically in the text.

Chapter 2. From Typology to Typography

1 Erich Auerbach, *Mimesis: The Representation of Reality in Western Literature,* trans. Willard R. Trask (Princeton: Princeton Univ. Press, 1953) 551, hereafter cited parenthetically in the text.

2 Hayden White, "The Interpretation of Texts," *Berkshire Review,* 19 (1984):17–18.

3 Brook Thomas, *James Joyce's Ulysses: A Book of Many Happy Returns* (Baton Rouge: Louisiana Univ. Press, 1982) 14.

4 Whereas "the story of Christ, with its ruthless mixture of everyday reality and the highest and most sublime tragedy" (*Mimesis* 555), is largely responsible for the medieval mixture of styles, it has nothing to do with the mixture of styles in modern realism, which Auerbach attributes to the French Revolution.

5 Erich Auerbach, "Figura," trans. Ralph Manheim, in *Scenes from the Drama of European Literature* (New York: Meridian Books, 1959) 72, hereafter cited parenthetically in the text.

6 See J. N. D. Kelly, *Early Christian Doctrines* (San Francisco: Harper & Row, 1978) 70, 73–74, hereafter cited parenthetically in the text.

7 Naomi Schor, *Reading in Detail: Aesthetics and the Feminine* (New York: Methuen, 1987) 46, hereafter cited parenthetically in the text.

8 Chrysostomos also turns up in "Circe" as one of the "eight male yellow and white children" Bloom bears after embracing Mrs. Thornton (*U* 403). Gifford and Seidman point out that Joyce's "Chrysostomos" may refer to the Greek rhetorician Dion Chrysostomos (the word means "golden-mouthed" in Greek) as well as to St. John Chrysostomos, "one of the Fathers of the early Church and Patriarch at Constantinople" (Don Gifford with Robert J. Seidman, *Notes For Joyce* [New York: E. P. Dutton, 1974] 7, hereafter cited parenthetically in the text as *NJ*).

9 D. W. Robertson, Jr., *A Preface to Chaucer: Studies in Medieval Perspectives* (Princeton: Princeton Univ. Press, 1962) 56.

10 An entire book dedicated to this idea has been produced: Sheldon Brivic, *Joyce the Creator* (Madison: Univ. of Wisconsin Press, 1985).

11 Brendan O Hehir suggested this reading to me.

12 Roland Barthes, *Criticism and Truth,* trans. and ed. Katrine Pilcher Keuneman (Minneapolis: Univ. of Minnesota Press, 1987) 68.

13 Hugh Kenner, *Ulysses* (London: Allen & Unwin, 1980) 155, 141.

14 Virginia Moseley, *Joyce and the Bible* (De Kalb: Northern Illinois Univ. Press, 1967) 130.

15 The Old and New Testaments fuse again at the end of "Cyclops," based loosely on the Transfiguration. Joyce even prepares typologically for this moment in the text. In the Bible it is the prophet Malachi who, in the last book of the Old Testament, promises the coming of Elijah: "Behold, I will send you Elijah the prophet before the coming of the great and dreadful day of the Lord" (Mal. 4:5). In "Scylla and Charybdis," Malachi Mulligan announces, "The Lord has spoken to Malachi" (*U* 175), echoing the scriptural phrase "The burden of the word of the Lord to Israel by Malachi" (Mal. 1:1); and sprinkled throughout (for the most part) the first half of *Ulysses* is the phrase "Elijah is coming," Joyce's equivalent to Malachi's prediction. Fulfillment occurs at the end of "Cyclops," which unites Moses, who appears solely in the guise of language—"The jarvey saved his life by furious driving as sure as God made Moses" (*U* 282)—Elijah, and Christ. (A "second coming" of Elijah takes place in "Circe" [*U* 414–15].) The scene superimposes the Transfiguration of Christ onto the Ascension of Elijah. (Moseley notes the way Joyce works Moses into this scene, and sees Joyce's telescoping of Elijah and Jesus "so that Elijah's translation into heaven may correspond to Jesus' ascension" [110].)

16 This Latin is from John 19:24, where the soldiers divide up Christ's garments among themselves and decide not to rend Christ's coat but to cast lots for it "that the scripture might be fulfilled, which saith, They parted my raiment among them, and for my vesture they did cast lots." The "scripture" referred to is Psalms 22:18.

17 Michael Groden, *Ulysses in Progress* (Princeton: Princeton Univ. Press, 1977) 167, 199, 200.

18 Groden, for example, apprehends the pattern and employs the vocabulary of typology in speaking of what he calls the "subheads" of "Aeolus": "The subheads foreshadow not only the succession of parody styles in 'Oxen of the Sun,' as Gilbert suggests, but all the voices—distinct both from the characters and from the narrators of the early episodes—who tell the story in the second half of the book" (113). Karen Lawrence writes that "what happens on a narrative level in later chapters is anticipated on the level of character at the beginning. . . ." (See her examples which follow this assertion.) Also: "In some ways, the general tone and feeling of the book and some of the narrative strategies of the later chapters are . . . predicted in the book's first half." For instance: "The verbal antics in 'Aeolus' adumbrate the play of language in subsequent chapters"; "the sturdy

trousers that salute the viceregal procession at the end of 'Wandering Rocks' . . . anticipate the gesturing objects of 'Circe.' " See Karen Lawrence, *The Odyssey of Style in Ulysses* (Princeton: Princeton Univ. Press, 1981) 13, 52, 70, 149–50.

19 Kenner, *Joyce's Voices* (Berkeley: Univ. of California Press, 1978) 116–17.

20 Stephen Greenblatt, *Renaissance Self-Fashioning: From More to Shakespeare* (Chicago: Univ. of Chicago Press, 1980) 213–14, 294.

21 The phrase "virgin womb of the imagination" appears in *A Portrait* (217) and "womb of imagination" in *Selected Letters* (202).

22 Northrop Frye, *The Great Code: The Bible and Literature* (New York: Harcourt, Brace, Jovanovich, 1982) 206, 208, 209.

23 J. Hillis Miller, "The Fiction of Realism," in *Dickens Centennial Essays*, ed. Ada Nisbet and Blake Nevius (Berkeley: Univ. of California Press, 1971) 124.

24 Frye 174.

25 Groden 54.

26 Frye 199.

27 Kenner 92.

28 David Simpson, *Fetishism and Imagination: Dickens, Melville, Conrad* (Baltimore: Johns Hopkins Univ. Press, 1982) 22. Simpson is quoting John Gordon's *Occasional Thoughts on the Study and Character of Classical Authors, on the Course of Litterature, and the Present Plan of a Learned Education, with Some Incidental Comparisons between Homer and Ossian* 56.

29 Kenner, "The *Portrait* in Perspective," in *A Portrait* 418.

30 Kenner, *Joyce's Voices* 41.

31 Carolyn G. Heilbrun, "Afterword," in *Women in Joyce*, ed. Suzette Henke and Elaine Unkeless (Urbana: Univ. of Illinois Press, 1982) 215.

32 Derek Attridge and Daniel Ferrer, "Introduction: Highly continental evenements," in *Post-structuralist Joyce: Essays from the French*, ed. Attridge and Ferrer (London: Cambridge Univ. Press, 1984) 7–8.

33 Attridge and Ferrer 10.

Chapter 3. Rose Upon the Rood of Time

1 Jacques Derrida, "Structure, Sign, and Play in the Discourse of the Human Sciences," in *The Languages of Criticism and the Sciences*

of Man: The Structuralist Controversy, ed. Richard Macksey and Eugenio Donato (Baltimore: Johns Hopkins Univ. Press, 1970) 252.

2 Richard Ellmann, *Ulysses on the Liffey* (New York: Oxford Univ. Press, 1972) 169.

3 From this point on, I will focus on bread and *blood* imagery since blood stands out over wine in the novel.

4 Tindall initiated the process of sacramentalizing Stephen and Bloom's imbibing of "Epps's massproduct, the creature cocoa" (William York Tindall, *James Joyce: His Way of Interpreting the Modern World* [New York: Charles Scribner's Sons, 1950] 29). Tindall, Cixous, and Ellmann stress Bloom's consecration of himself as a secular host in a tub-chalice (Tindall, *A Reader's Guide to James Joyce* [London: Thames & Hudson, 1959] 156; Hélène Cixous, *The Exile of James Joyce,* trans. Sally A. J. Purcell [New York: David Lewis, 1972] 118; Ellmann, *Liffey* 43). Ellmann notes a parallel between Gerty and the sacrament (*Liffey* 128).

5 David Simpson, *Fetishism and Imagination: Dickens, Melville, Conrad* (Baltimore: Johns Hopkins Univ. Press, 1982) 12. Simpson quotes here J. A. Dulaure, *Histoire abrégée de differens cultes* (1825)1:27.

6 Jacques Derrida, *Spurs: Nietzsche's Styles,* trans. Barbara Harlow (Chicago: Univ. of Chicago Press, 1978) 55.

7 See Ellmann, *Liffey* 170–71.

8 In Leviticus, for example, we read: "And if any man lie with her at all, and her flowers be upon him, he shall be unclean seven days; and all the bed whereon he lieth shall be unclean" (Lev. 15:24). This chapter of Leviticus concludes with: "This is the law of . . . her that is sick of her flowers . . . and of him that lieth with her that is unclean" (Lev. 15:32–33).

9 I use the Fathers of the English Dominican Province translation of the *Summa:* St. Thomas Aquinas, *The Summa Theologica,* trans. Fathers of the English Dominican Province (New York: Benziger Brothers, 1947), hereafter cited parenthetically in the text as *ST.* Stephen's three questions come from Aquinas's discussion in *ST,* III, Q. 76, Art. 2; *ST,* III, Q. 76, Art. 3; and *ST,* III, Q. 77, Art. 4. The questions Aquinas deals with are: "Whether the Whole Christ Is Contained under Each Species of This Sacrament?" "Whether Christ Is Entire under Every Part of the Species of the Bread and Wine?" and "Whether the Sacramental Species Can Be Corrupted?"

10 Edward Schillebeeckx, O.P., *The Eucharist,* trans. N. D. Smith (New York: Sheed and Ward, 1968) 11–15.

11 Joseph M. Powers, S.J., *Eucharistic Theology* (New York: Herder and Herder, 1967) 116, 118.

12 Buck can even be identified with the Reverend Love: Father Boyle points out that in describing George Moore's clerical character in *The Lake*—a character Moore named after Gogarty—Joyce said to Stanislaus, "Father Oliver Gogarty goes out to the lake to plunge in by moonlight, before which the moon shines opportunely 'on a firm erect frame and grey buttocks' " (Robert Boyle, S.J., "The Priesthoods of Stephen and Buck," in *Approaches to Ulysses*, ed. Thomas F. Staley and Bernard Benstock [Pittsburgh: Univ. of Pittsburgh Press, 1970] 59).

13 William York Tindall, *Reader's Guide* 216.

14 Tindall 222.

15 R. Howard Bloch, "Medieval Misogyny," *Representations*, special issue "Misogyny, Misandry, and Misanthropy," ed. R. Howard Bloch and Frances Ferguson, 20 (1987):15, 19.

16 Walter J. Ong, S.J., "Wit and Mystery: A Revaluation in Mediaeval Latin Hymnody," *Speculum*, 22 (1947):316–17.

17 Ong 317, 318.

18 Bloch 11, 14, 20.

Chapter 4. The Parturition of the Word

1 E. H. Gombrich, *Art and Illusion: A Study in the Psychology of Pictorial Representation* (Princeton: Princeton Univ. Press, 1956) 112–13.

2 Leo Manglaviti, "Joyce and St. John," *James Joyce Quarterly*, 9 (1971):152.

3 Mary Colum and Padraic Colum, *Our Friend James Joyce* (Garden City, New York: Doubleday, 1958) 182.

4 Richard Ellmann, *Ulysses on the Liffey* (New York: Oxford Univ. Press, 1972) 1–2.

5 Kenneth Burke, *The Rhetoric of Religion: Studies in Logology* (Boston: Beacon Press, 1961) 2.

6 William York Tindall, *A Reader's Guide to James Joyce* (London: Thames & Hudson, 1959) 216. Ellmann and Boyle also acknowledge this trinity.

7 See Ralph Rader, "Exodus and Return: Joyce's *Ulysses* and the Fiction of the Actual," *University of Toronto Quarterly*, 48 (1978–79):164–65.

8 Ellmann, *Liffey* 153–54.

9 Robert Boyle, S.J., *James Joyce's Pauline Vision: A Catholic Exposition* (Carbondale: Southern Illinois Univ. Press, 1978) 19–20.

10 Edward Said, *Beginnings: Intention and Method* (Baltimore: Johns Hopkins Univ. Press, 1975) 83.

11 See both William T. Noon, S.J., *Joyce and Aquinas* (New Haven: Yale Univ. Press, 1957) 118–19, and Boyle 82.

12 Burke 7.

13 Noon 119.

14 See R. L. Richard, "Holy Trinity," *New Catholic Encyclopedia*, 1967 ed., vol. 14, 303.

15 See Noon 25–26.

16 Karen Lawrence, *The Odyssey of Style in Ulysses* (Princeton: Princeton Univ. Press, 1981) 63.

17 Said xiii.

18 I adopt here Bakhtin's concepts of the "centripetal" and "centrifugal," which Holquist defines in the glossary of *The Dialogic Imagination* as "respectively the centralizing and decentralizing (or decentering) forces in any language or culture" (M. M. Bakhtin, *The Dialogic Imagination*, ed. Michael Holquist, trans. Caryl Emerson and Michael Holquist [Austin: Univ. of Texas Press, 1981] 425).

19 Mark Shechner, *Joyce in Nighttown: A Psychoanalytic Inquiry into Ulysses* (Berkeley: Univ. of California Press, 1974) 22.

20 Nathaniel Hawthorne, *The Centenary Edition of the Works of Nathaniel Hawthorne*, ed. William Charvat et al. (Columbus: Ohio State Univ. Press, 1962), 1:10, hereafter cited parenthetically in the text as *SL*.

21 Simpson reads Dickens as a critic of "the fetishized imagination, as it results in a topsy-turvy world wherein all authentic relations are inverted or excluded. This world is an energetic mechanism, the perpetual friction between the uncoordinated parts never creating anything whole" (xiv). If a name in Dickens calls attention to itself, "it suggests that the outward sign has usurped the inner being, which is thus effaced from all acts of valorization and exchange" (53). See David Simpson, *Fetishism and Imagination: Dickens, Melville, Conrad* (Baltimore: Johns Hopkins Univ. Press, 1982) 58.

22 Simpson 21.

23 Tony Tanner, *City of Words* (New York: Harper & Row, 1971) 23.

24 Simpson 17.

25 Simpson 21. Simpson is quoting John Gordon's *Occasional Thoughts on the Study and Character of Classical Authors, on the Course of*

Litterature, and the Present Plan of a Learned Education, with Some Incidental Comparisons between Homer and Ossian 39–40.

Chapter 5. *"Petticoat Government"*

1 Gilles Deleuze, *Masochism: An Interpretation of Coldness and Cruelty* together with *Venus in Furs* by Leopold von Sacher-Masoch, trans. Jean McNeil from French trans. by Aude Willm (New York: George Braziller, 1971) 13, hereafter cited parenthetically in the text as *M* and *VF.*

2 Shechner was probably the first to emphasize Joyce's urge to mold Nora into a Venus in Furs (Mark Shechner, *Joyce in Nighttown: A Psychoanalytic Inquiry into Ulysses* [Berkeley: Univ. of California Press, 1974] 65–70). In general, Shechner's study is a Freudian analysis of much of the same material I read primarily in a Deleuzean mode.

3 See Sigmund Freud, "Fetishism," in *The Standard Edition of the Complete Psychological Works of Sigmund Freud,* trans. James Strachey, vol. 21 (London: Hogarth Press, 1927) 152–57.

4 Gilles Deleuze and Félix Guattari, *Anti-Oedipus: Capitalism and Schizophrenia,* trans. Robert Hurley, Mark Seem, and Helena R. Lane (New York: Viking Press, 1977) 61.

5 James Joyce, *Giacomo Joyce* (New York: Viking Press, 1968) xi, 1, hereafter cited parenthetically in the text as *GJ.*

6 James Cleugh, *The First Masochist: A Biography of Leopold von Sacher-Masoch* (London: Anthony Blond, 1967) 167–68.

7 See Shechner 116–17, 150, 251–52.

8 See Deleuze's chap. 9, "Psychoanalysis and the Problem of Masochism," for a discussion of the differences between Freud's and Deleuze's conceptions of masochism. Freud (and not Deleuze) believes that the masochist identifies "with the mother and offers himself to the father as a sexual object; however, since this would in turn renew the threat of castration which he is trying to avert, he chooses 'being beaten' both as exorcism of 'being castrated' and as a regressive substitute of 'being loved'; at the same time the mother takes on the role of the person who beats, as a result of repression of the homosexual choice" (*M* 92–93). See also Sigmund Freud, "The Economic Problem of Masochism," in *The Standard Edition of the Complete Psychological Works of Sigmund Freud,* trans. James Strachey, vol. 19 (London: Hogarth Press, 1924) 159–70, and Sigmund Freud, "A Child is Being Beaten," in ibid., vol. 27 (1919) 179–204.

9 It is worth noting, however, partly to account for the comic nature of Joyce's contract with Molly, that in masochism "the contract is caricatured." Deleuze writes: "In the contractual relation the woman typically figures as an object in the patriarchal system. The contract in masochism reverses this state of affairs by making the woman into the party with whom the contract is entered into. . . . [I]t involves a master-slave relationship . . . in which the woman is master and torturer. The contractual basis is thereby implicitly challenged, by excess of zeal, a humorous acceleration of the clauses and a complete reversal of the respective contractual status of man and woman" (*M* 80).

10 Christine van Boheemen, *The Novel as Family Romance: Language, Gender, and Authority from Fielding to Joyce* (Ithaca: Cornell Univ. Press, 1987) 177, hereafter cited parenthetically in the text as *NFR*. It should be noted that this is one step within a larger, complicated feminist argument, which in several respects overlaps with my own. For example, Boheemen writes that "Molly Bloom . . . has the power of the word, which turns her into Joyce's—no less than Bloom's—agent of vengeance against masculine rivals and castrating females alike" (181).

11 Roland Barthes, "From Work to Text," in *Image Music Text,* trans. Stephen Heath (New York: Hill and Wang, 1977) 159.

12 Alice A. Jardine, *Gynesis: Configurations of Woman and Modernity* (Ithaca: Cornell Univ. Press, 1985) 25.

13 In correspondence, Fritz Senn called my attention to the aggressiveness of "pun" by pointing out that it can mean "pound," as in *Troilus and Cressida,* II, i.

14 Jane Gallop, *The Daughter's Seduction: Feminism and Psychoanalysis* (Ithaca: Cornell Univ. Press, 1982) 47.

15 Stephen Heath, "Male Feminism," in *Men in Feminism,* ed. Alice Jardine and Paul Smith (New York: Methuen, 1987) 27.

16 Jardine 38.

17 It should be noted that Sandra Gilbert argues (in a way that intersects with, but that certainly has different stress points from, my Deleuzean position) against a feminist interpretation of the Nighttown episode. Focusing more on Bloom than on Joyce, Gilbert adopts Robert Stoller's theory that "the male transvestite uses the degrading apparatus of female costume to convert 'humiliation' to 'mastery' by showing himself (and the world) that he is not 'just' like a woman, he is better than a woman because he is a woman with a penis." Bloom is saved "from the depravations of Bella/Bello Cohen by not only having but ironically pretending to *be* his own *Molly,* a covertly

but triumphantly phallic version of the recumbent *Ewig-Weibliche*, a 'new womanly man' . . . whose secret manliness must ultimately co-opt *and* conquer all insubordinate 'new women.' " See Sandra M. Gilbert, "Costumes of the Mind: Transvestism as Metaphor in Modern Literature," in *Writing and Sexual Difference*, ed. Elizabeth Abel (Chicago: Univ. of Chicago Press, 1982) 199, 201. In a reading of "Circe" less compatible (than Gilbert's) with my own, Richard Brown in *Joyce and Sexuality* regards Joyce's and his male characters' attraction to dominant women as part of Joyce's feminism. With this conclusion, Brown not only misses the complicated inner strategic motives of masochism but, on a simple level, glosses over many of his own statements testifying to Joyce's misogyny: Joyce insisted on "the sexuality of women according to his brother's disapproving diary record of 1904. 'Jim says he has an instinct for women,' [Stanislaus] writes. 'He scarcely ever talks decently of them even those he likes. He talks as of warm, soft-skinned animals. 'That one'd give you a great push!' 'She's very warm between the thighs, I fancy.' 'She has a great action, I'm sure'." See Richard Brown, *James Joyce and Sexuality* (Cambridge: Cambridge Univ. Press, 1985) 116, especially chap. 3, "Women."

18 Robert Boyle, S.J., "Penelope," in *James Joyce's Ulysses: Critical Essays,* ed. Clive Hart and David Hayman (Berkeley: Univ. of California Press, 1974) 416.

19 Jacques Lacan, "The signification of the phallus," in *Ecrits,* trans. Alan Sheridan (New York: W.W. Norton, 1977) 287.

20 Julia Kristeva, *Desire in Language: A Semiotic Approach to Literature and Art,* ed. Leon Roudiez, trans. Thomas Gora, Alice Jardine, and Leon S. Roudiez (New York: Columbia Univ. Press, 1980) 157, hereafter cited parenthetically in the text as *DL.*

21 *Oxford English Dictionary,* 1971 ed., 1833, 1749.

22 Robert Boyle, S.J., makes this observation in "Penelope," in *James Joyce's Ulysses: Critical Essays,* 429. He also notes that Molly "shares a name and a birthday with the Blessed Virgin" (422); and he reads the number eight in the chapter as a symbol of "Molly's genital area" (412).

23 Boyle 408.

24 Jacques Derrida, *Spurs: Nietzsche's Styles,* trans. Barbara Harlow (Chicago: Univ. of Chicago Press, 1978) 59.

25 Derrida 39.

26 Gayatri Chakravorty Spivak, "Displacement and the Discourse of Woman," in *Displacement: Derrida and After*, ed. Mark Krupnick (Bloomington: Indiana Univ. Press, 1983) 170, 184.

27 Julia Kristeva, "Stabat Mater," in *The Kristeva Reader*, ed. Toril Moi, trans. Leon S. Roudiez (New York: Columbia Univ. Press, 1986) 161–62.

28 Kristeva 162–63.

Index

189